Asian Christianity in the Diaspora

Series Editors
Grace Ji-Sun Kim
Earlham School of Religion
Richmond, IN, USA

Joseph Cheah
University of Saint Joseph
West Hartford, CT, USA

Asian American theology is still at its nascent stage. It began in the 1980's with just a handful of scholars who were recent immigrants to the United States. Now with the rise in Asian American population and the rise of Asian American theologians, this new community is an ever-important voice within theological discourse and Asian American cultural studies. This new series seeks to bring to the forefront some of the important, provocative new voices within Asian American Theology. The series aims to provide Asian American theological responses to the complex process of migration and resettlement process of Asian immigrants and refugees. We will address theoretical works on the meaning of diaspora, exile, and social memory, and the foundational works concerning the ways in which displaced communities remember and narrate their experiences. Such an interdisciplinary approach entails intersectional analysis between Asian American contextual theology and one other factor; be it sexuality, gender, race/ethnicity, and/or cultural studies. This series also addresses Christianity from Asian perspectives. We welcome manuscripts that examine the identity and internal coherence of the Christian faith in its encounters with different Asian cultures, with Asian people, the majority of whom are poor, and with non-Christian religions that predominate the landscape of the Asian continent. Palgrave is embarking on a transformation of discourse within Asian and Asian American theological scholarship as this will be the first of its kind. As we live in a global world in which Christianity has re-centered itself in the Global South and among the racialized minorities in the United States, it behooves us to listen to the rich, diverse and engaging voices of Asian and Asian American theologians.

More information about this series at
http://www.palgrave.com/gp/series/14781

Jung Eun Sophia Park · Emily S. Wu
Editors

Interreligous Pedagogy

Reflections and Applications in Honor
of Judith A. Berling

Editors
Jung Eun Sophia Park
Holy Names University
Oakland, CA, USA

Emily S. Wu
Dominican University of California
San Rafael, CA, USA

Asian Christianity in the Diaspora
ISBN 978-3-319-91505-0   ISBN 978-3-319-91506-7   (eBook)
https://doi.org/10.1007/978-3-319-91506-7

Library of Congress Control Number: 2018941871

Cover illustration: © Melisa Hasan

Printed on acid-free paper

This Palgrave Pivot imprint is published by the registered company Springer International Publishing AG part of Springer Nature
The registered company address is: Gewerbestrasse 11, 6330 Cham, Switzerland

PRAISE FOR *INTERRELIGOUS PEDAGOGY*

"One of the biggest challenges in theological education today and for the fore-seeable future is interreligious engagement. Judith Berling's brilliant and mul-tifaceted career includes developing and practicing interreligious pedagogy that offers multiple ways in which to effectively transform challenges into opportuni-ties for greater understanding and appreciation of one another. This volume is a fitting tribute to the master teacher."
   —Uriah Y. Kim, *John Dillenberger Professor of Biblical Studies, Graduate Theological Union, USA*

"This collection of essays offers a rich introduction to Judith Berling's prac-tices of interreligious teaching and learning. Written by her students, the ideas reflected in each chapter are important in themselves, as embodied approaches to dialogue, interreligious pedagogy and interdisciplinary boundary crossing. I commend this book to all who are interested in new approaches to interreligious theological education and religious studies."
   —Philip L. Wickeri, *Advisor to the Archbishop on Historical and Theological Studies, Hong Kong Sheng Kung Hui (Anglican Church)*

PREFACE

When I came to the Graduate Theological Union as Dean in 1987, I left behind my thirteen years of teaching Religious Studies and East Asian Studies at Indiana University, Bloomington. At Indiana University, I taught a broad spectrum of students: undergraduates in general education courses, majors in East Asian Studies and in Religious Studies, honors courses, and master's- and doctoral-level courses. During those years, I fell in love with teaching as a profession, even as I struggled as a novice professor to master the art of engaging and listening to students, bringing out their ideas and voices. I was thus broken-hearted that my duties as Dean of the GTU kept me away from the classroom for eight years; I could not do justice to my administrative responsibilities and also develop and teach new graduate-level courses.

When I finally reentered the classroom in the late 1990s, I discovered that the hiatus had been a blessing. My long break from classroom teaching gave me an opportunity to start afresh, but with the benefit of experience: I was able to distance myself from the traditional approaches of forbears who had been my early models, and to embrace more fully feminist and student-centered approaches that I had previously tried to insert gradually into older models of pedagogy, with mixed results. I finally began to come into my own as a teacher.

I credit my pedagogical development largely to my students, who challenged me on two fronts: (1) to develop a teaching course for GTU doctoral students and (2) to develop a seminar on interdisciplinary research for doctoral students in interdisciplinary studies. In response to these student requests, I developed the two courses that best honed my pedagogical principles and approaches: Seminar on Course Design and Syllabus Development, and Seminar on Interdisciplinarity. The seminars, which I taught annually, stretched and challenged me pedagogically, but—even more important—I learned deeply with and from the students who took them. They were powerfully collaborative learning environments for me as teacher, mentor, and scholar, and for the students, who were discovering their gifts as scholars and teachers. These seminars were learning laboratories for students to articulate and explore the approaches they would use in their teaching and their scholarship.

When GTU approached me about an event to celebrate my retirement, I asked that it be focused on the work of my students. The resulting two-day conference was a wonderful celebration of the achievements of GTU and its graduates, and it was a joy for me to see the outstanding work that they were doing. Nothing could be more satisfying than to see how those whom you have taught take the small seeds that you may have given them and produce rich and wonderful gardens of ideas. I am still learning from and with them, exploring how to cross the many borders that impede mutual understanding.

Berkeley, CA, USA   Judith A. Berling

ACKNOWLEDGEMENTS

This book is the fruit of a symposium that was held to celebrate Judith Berling's academic contributions. We would like to acknowledge the support of Graduate Theological Union (GTU) in making the symposium possible. The President Riess Pottervelt and former Academic Dean Arthur Holder, as the steering committee, were involved in every step of the two-year planning process. The excellent and creative crew at GTU, most notably Teresa Joye, Angela Muñoz, Christopher Cox, and Kyle Schiefelbein, provided much administrative, organizational, and technical support with generous hearts. Special thanks to Munir Jiwa, who not only participated in dialogue but also provided essential operational support for the symposium through the Center for Islamic Studies.

We are grateful to Judith's colleagues, students, and friends, many of whom traveled from around the world and participated in the symposium. We are exceedingly grateful to those who engaged profoundly in the dialogue, but whose intellectual brilliance we were not able to include in this edited volume: Philip Wickeri, Jenny Te Paa-Daniel, Fumitaka Matsuoka, Damayanthi Niles, Devin Zuber, Matthew Haar Farris (TwoTree), Yik Fai Tam, Elizabeth Ingenthron, Norris Palmer, John Thompson, Kanghack Lee, and Reem Javed.

We would like to also thank our series editors Joe Cheah and Grace Ji-Sun Kim for their support and guidance. We also thank Levi

Checketts, Nina Hunt, and Sheila Gibson for their editorial assistance through thoughtful readings.

Last but not least, we thank Judith from the bottom of our hearts for being an amazing teacher, mentor, ally, advocate, and friend.

CONTENTS

NOTES ON CONTRIBUTORS

Judith A. Berling is Professor of Chinese and comparative religions at Graduate Theological Union (GTU). Berling previously was dean and vice president of GTU from 1987 to 1996. In addition, Berling served as Director of Incarnating Globalization, a project of the Association of Theological Schools, from 1996 to 2000. Among her many honors are the Herman Bachman Lieber Distinguished Teaching Award at Indiana University in 1986, the Sarlo Excellence in Teaching Award at GTU in 2003, the Ray L. Hart Service Award from the American Academy of Religion in 2005, and her selection as the GTU Distinguished Faculty Lecturer in 2000. Berling was president of the American Academy of Religion from 1990 to 1991 and is a past president of the American Society for the Study of Religions (2002–2005). She is a past trustee and vice chair of the United Board for Christian Higher Education in Asia, a founding co-editor of Teaching Theology and Religion, and a member of the Association of Theological Schools Commission on Accreditation (1988–1994, chair in 1994).

Courtney Bruntz is Assistant Professor of Asian Religions at Doane University in Crete, Nebraska. She received her Ph.D. from the Graduate Theological Union, under the mentorship of Judith Berling. At present, her research analyzes Buddhist teachings and practices in contemporary China, taking place in both urban and rural settings.

Joanne Doi MM, PhD taught at the Franciscan School of Theology in Berkeley, CA as assistant professor of intercultural theologies and ministries before coming to Chicago, IL to serve as Co-director of the Maryknoll Sisters Integration Program; previously, she served in Peru among the Aymara people. She currently teaches at the Catholic Theological Union.

Elizabeth Stanhope Gordon combines a legal background with research in spirituality and religion, cognitive science, and cultural anthropology. She has applied her research on spirituality to behavioral health recovery, youth substance abuse prevention, administrative management in multicultural settings, leadership development, and social justice awareness. She currently teaches for Seattle University.

Bonnie Howe is an Affiliated Professor of Social Ethics and Biblical Interpretation at New College Berkeley, an affiliate of Graduate Theological Union. She uses cognitive linguistic theories and methods to analyze moral discourse. Publications include *Because You Bear This Name: Metaphor and the Moral Meaning of 1 Peter* (Society of Biblical Literature, 2008) and *Cognitive Linguistic Explorations in Biblical Studies* (De Gruyter, 2014).

Jung Eun Sophia Park is Associate Professor in religious studies at the Holy Names University. She is the author of numerous books, including *Dislocation as Experience: Creating a Hybrid Identity, Constructing a Borderland* (Peter Lang, 2010), and *Border Crossing Spirituality: Transformation in Borderland* (PickWick, 2016). Her research interest is global women's spirituality and cross-cultural spiritual direction.

Ofelia O. Villero has been a qualitative research specialist at University of California, San Francisco, since 2007. She specializes in health disparities research with vulnerable populations, in particular women of color, immigrants, and older adults. Her research includes the following areas: breast cancer, diabetes, cardiovascular diseases, music and aging, and medication adherence.

Emily S. Wu teaches in the Religion Department and Service-Learning Program at Dominican University of California. She is the author of *Traditional Chinese Medicine in the United States: Searching for Spiritual Meaning and Ultimate Health* (Lexington, 2013). Her primary research interests are food, healing, and medical practices in Chinese and other East Asian religious contexts. Wu's teaching and community work also explore deeply into the diasporic, transnational, and cross-cultural Asian experiences and understandings of health and healing, community-building, and social justice.

LIST OF FIGURES

CHAPTER 1

Introduction

Jung Eun Sophia Park and Emily S. Wu

Abstract Judith Berling's interpersonal pedagogy can be summarized as a mutual teaching and learning process in which various ways of boundary crossing can occur. Berling's model empowers learners by providing a safe space to explore their own quest. Also, this chapter introduces each chapter's contents, which deepens, critiques, applies as well as appreciates and appropriates Judith Berling's pedagogy. Furthermore, the chapter explores how each intersects and shares certain themes with the others as a way of examining Berling's engaging pedagogy, which is by nature boundary crossing and interdisciplinary.

Keywords Inter-religious · Engaging teaching and learning model Boundary-crossing · Interdisciplinary approach · Encounter

Inter-religious education is often equated to interfaith dialogue as a process of learning non-Christian religions by crossing the boundaries of Christian understanding. The supposed benefit of inter-religious studies

J. E. S. Park (✉)
Holy Names University, Oakland, CA, USA

E. S. Wu
Dominican University of California, San Rafael, CA, USA

© The Author(s) 2018
J. E. S. Park and E. S. Wu (eds.), *Interreligous Pedagogy*, Asian Christianity in the Diaspora, https://doi.org/10.1007/978-3-319-91506-7_1

1

is to help refine or redefine Christian identity and, hopefully, understand the other. In today's multicultural and secular society, however, teaching and learning religions is much more complex than negotiating or affirming Christian faith and identities. There is, of course, the desire for wisdom and knowledge given by religion and spirituality, including a transcendental level of transformation. Students are also interested in how religions, as sources of wisdom, can provide critical perspectives for understanding social phenomena and the relationship to the students' lives as well as how they can provide appropriate tools to address problems of the world in terms of social justice and peace. Additionally, scholars and educators must acknowledge the diverse and intersectional realities that the students, or all of us, experience.

Judith Berling's engaging mutual teaching and learning model is most celebrated for its focus on and effectiveness in boundary-crossing. Crossing boundaries actually occurs at all levels of Berling's personal and professional life. The crossing is manifest through her noting that she wanted to learn *about* the Chinese culture as well as learn *from* the Chinese culture.[1] When she moved from Indiana University in 1987 to serve as the Academic Dean of the Graduate Theological Union in Berkeley, California, her boundary-crossing pedagogy became a signature model for the many scholars trained at the school. More specifically, her seminars on interdisciplinarity and course design became the seminal courses through which she guided doctoral students' interdisciplinary understanding of boundary-crossings, developing their scholarly adventures. She has also taught and advised students from a wide range of ethnic, cultural, disciplinary, and professional backgrounds and has transmitted a deep sense of bliss with regard to learning with and from her students.

This book originated from a conference held in Berkeley, California, in 2016 that honored Berling's influential work in teaching and pedagogy. Her colleagues, friends, and former students gathered from all over the world to share their thoughts, discussing critical elements of boundary-crossing in Judith Berling's inter-religious and engaging philosophy. The conference participants committed to continuing the conversations and elaborating on the various applications of Berling's approach. Throughout the process, chapter authors of this collection participated

---

[1]Judith Berling, *A Pilgrim in Chinese Culture: Negotiation Religious Diversity* (Maryknoll, NY: Orbis Books, 2002), 22.

in dialogue with one another as well as with Judith Berling herself. We experienced a transformation and extension of our understanding following her cooperative learning model.

All chapters in this book are firmly grounded in and inspired by Judith Berling's pedagogy. Somewhat serendipitously, chapter authors all pay tribute to Berling's seminal work, *Understanding Other Religious Worlds: A Guide for Interreligious Education*.[2] In other words, the book, fondly referred to by Berling's students and colleagues as "The Purple Book" (due to its purple book cover), functions as the main framework in this edited volume.

In *Understanding Other Religious Worlds*, Berling identifies five threads in inter-religious teaching and learning: (1) encountering difference or entering other worlds; (2) responding from one's own location; (3) conducting conversation and dialogue; (4) developing relationships; and (5) internalizing the process.[3] The five threads include and emphasize the value of mutual respect and conversation. In practice, Berling engages in dialogue with various feminist educators and inspirational thinkers such as Maxine Greene and bell hook, as well as with her colleagues, parishioners, and students. Berling further elaborates that the consequences of the five threads are situated between two poles: "(1) understanding the other religion faithfully and (2) re-appropriating Christian tradition in light of new understandings and relationships."[4] In this way, learners can extend and deepen their understanding across boundaries as they allow themselves to engage and transform.

Furthermore, Berling explicitly identifies six principles of boundary-crossing learning: "(1) building on the diversity of learners' experiences; (2) empowering learners through developing their voice and agency; (3) [imaginatively] entering other worlds through arts, text, or narrative; (4) engaging, understanding, and interpreting the distinctive ways in which religions represent themselves; (5) developing [mediating or translating] linguistic flexibility through mutually critical conversations; and (6) establishing mutually respectful relationships, learning to stand with others."[5]

---

[2] Judith Berling, *Understanding Other Religious Worlds: A Guide for Interrreligious Education* (Maryknoll, NY: Orbis Books, 2004).

[3] Ibid., 64–79.

[4] Ibid., 71.

[5] Ibid., 63.

These principles address the need to recognize the role of imagination and interpretation that are involved in the learning process, regardless of context or discipline. Additionally, embedded in these principles is a social justice imperative to understand one's own position with its privileges and restrictions. In her pedagogy, the core value of border-crossing, which emphasizes the notion of "right relationship," unfolds to the extent that the subject becomes the object or the subject takes a position of the "other."

If we only consider the academic framework only, our understanding of Berling's pedagogy would be too narrow and limited. To understand her pedagogy, which aims for spiritual transformation, it is essential to pay attention to the concept of friendship and hospitality. Regarding this aspect, Berling's *A Pilgrim in Chinese Culture: Negotiating Religious Diversity* can be a guide.[6] In this book, Berling investigates how to create a safe space for searching for the truth, which we assume that engaging the other entails. Genuine respect and humility, which often is attuned to attentive listening, can be keys for learners to encounter other religions and experience transformation.

Since all the chapter authors were Berling's students and advisees, her pedagogical theories are recognized and advanced in every chapter. Staying consistent to Berling's usual interactive and responsive scholarship, Berling herself responds in the concluding chapter.

Taking the lead is Jung Eun Sophia Park's chapter, which explores the characteristics of Nones—those who are not affiliated with any institutionalized religion yet who desire spiritual growth or a more spiritual feeling—through an analysis of literature on Nones. Park demonstrates three models of epistemology of other religions, paying attention to postcolonial theory as well as Jacques Lacan's concept of gaze for Nones. For these Nones, Park suggests an inverted process of teaching that is structured on students' own interests and questions. The author emphasizes the flexibility of teachers to change curriculum by paying attention to the learning process of the students rather than simply adhering to their fixed teaching plans. This chapter strongly argues that Berling's model should be utilized and revisited as a new way of education for Nones.

In Chapter 3, Ofelia O. Villero narrates her personal story of how Judith Berling's model of teaching and learning helped her cross

---

[6]Judith Berling, *A Pilgrim in Chinese Culture: Negotiating Religious Diversity* (Maryknoll, NY: Orbis Books, 2002).

disciplines from religious studies to health sciences in a time when the humanities, and religious studies in particular, are under siege. In this way, her personal narrative intersects with her professional one. Villero also elaborates on how Berling's notion of the learning process of religion can be applied to a non-religious context through the author's qualitative participatory action research project. As a venue for "right relationship" between researcher and informants, Villero emphasizes the notion of race and gender in designing research. The author, as a community-based participatory health researcher, emphasizes that Berling's mentorship and articulation of the learning process made it possible for her to enter other worlds through engaging and crossing boundaries of significant difference and, along the way, develop her own voice and those of others.

Emily S. Wu demonstrates in Chapter 4 that, building upon Berling's model of teaching and learning, cultural boundaries can be effectively crossed through narratives. More specifically, when people are provided with a safe space to retell their life experiences in their own voices, not only are the storytellers empowered to teach about their lives, but learners are also empowered to participate in the process of knowledge production by documenting the stories. With this framing, Wu's undergraduate students who take her service-learning courses use oral history collection as the platform to actively engage with Asian American elders in the community, as well as to practice the principles of accompaniment and cultural humility.

Courtney Bruntz provides in Chapter 5 strategies for educating students on how they can become active learners in the classroom, adapting Judith Berling's method for inter-religious education to the millennial generation. Bruntz introduces her teaching method, which she has found successful for creating environments of active learning within and outside the classroom space as well as for expanding students' understanding of other religions beyond stereotypical knowledge. Emphasizing the notion of "encounter" in her class, students enter other religious worlds through art, texts, and narratives and then continue their individualized learning by leading reflections upon such encounters. The author concludes that the engaged educational environments for inter-religious learning complement the learning styles of the millennial generation which can be characterized as creative seeking and collaborative.

In Chapter 6, Joanne Doi demonstrates how Judith Berling's teaching and learning model can empower learners, eloquently interweaving strands of personal, professional, and spiritual life. As a third-generation Japanese American and Maryknoll sister who spent her youth in Peru serving the indigenous people in Andes, she identifies as a border-crossing educator. Throughout her journey, Doi expresses how much Berling's pedagogy empowered her as an educator.

As an application of Berling's teaching and learning method, she introduces two graduate theological courses which Doi designed and taught at the Graduate Theological Union in Berkeley. The courses include a specific focus on the Asian Americans' immigration experiences and interpretation, emphasizing the interdisciplinary and dialogic nature of Berling's pedagogy of empowering learners. Doi describes the first course as a collaborative interdisciplinary course which engaged with three areas of critical studies including Scripture, collective memory, and the development of faith communities within Asian American immigration waves. The course itself was designed with a Biblical scholar so that the course was, by nature, interdisciplinary, and Doi stresses that the collaboration between two educators strengthened the learning process. The second course demonstrates a mutual learning pedagogy by emphasizing the co-learning environment on the Manzanar Pilgrimage, in which Japanese Americans experienced historical injury. In this journey, learners' community is fostered by relationality with respect to the topography of memory. The author explains how Berling's method, which focuses on empowering modes of epistemology, fosters intercultural understanding through her designed courses.

In Chapter 7, Elizabeth Stanhope Gordon expands on Berling's inter-religious approach in order to embrace the learning process of encountering difference for higher education students who identify as either religious or non-religious. She expands on this to incorporate a pedagogy which explicitly recognizes the transcendent or spiritual aspects of human experience outside of a religious framework. The author argues that a critical framework of spirituality, wisdom, and wisdom sharing should become an integral part of higher education curriculum development across disciplines.

As pluralism increases in our society, a greater need arises for appreciation and understanding of our common humanity. This expanded outlook allows for student growth in cross-cultural values, such as mutuality, compassion, empathy, and justice, as well as in increased awareness of religious and non-religious wisdom traditions that promote individual and communal well-being.

Bonnie Howe explores, in Chapter 8, how metaphors and conceptual frames guide, constrain, and validate the interdisciplinary study of religions. Howe's analysis of cognitive metaphors and conceptual frames illuminates the critical notions of overarching assumptions that the teachers embrace. She argues that the metaphors teachers utilize for describing the course and its topics, and the frames by which they convey contents of the course carry strong assumptions, and thus, teachers already impart these assumptions to the learners. Consequently, educators need to listen closely to the metaphors and frames that students bring to discussions and their written work, because these might be quite different from those of educators.

By attending to what these metaphors and frames suggest, educators can understand the locations/contexts/backgrounds/agenda of their learners and can learn to both understand and communicate with them better. In effect, when attention is paid to what students bring to the course, many different "worlds" reveal themselves, and the task then becomes to understand across difference through engaged and collaborative dialogue.

In the concluding final chapter, Judith Berling responds to these seven chapters by engaging with the contents brought up by the authors and in so doing extends her own inter-religious pedagogy, characterized as an engaging and empowering teaching and learning model.

Readers will find the chapters in this book interrelated and connected to one another. Some chapters share similar concerns, while some chapters organically respond to questions raised in other chapters. Those interactions among attributed authors occur in various ways.

The first set of shared concerns arises among those who teach undergraduate classes. Sophia Park, who teaches at a liberal art university in California, shares with Courtney Bruntz, who "flips" her Asian religions classroom in Nebraska, the concern about how to teach undergraduate students—millennials and the non-religious. Elizabeth Gordon proposes using the language of "wisdom sharing," and Emily Wu promotes using narratives as a focus of community engagement to create spaces for the empowerment of students. They demonstrate how Berling's pedagogy can be effectively and variably utilized at the undergraduate level.

Several chapter authors share concerns for the social process of "othering." Ofelia Villero reflects on her breast cancer research among

Filipino women, to reaffirm the implications of Orientalism and the danger of being "other" in American society. Joanne Doi's experience of teaching through pilgrimages to Japanese interment sites confronts a painful history of exclusion through reconciliation. Similarly, Emily Wu challenges the ongoing silencing of minority voices through her oral history collection project. All three of these chapters are situated in the Bay Area, where Asian and Asian American populations are high but not necessarily appreciated properly or treated fairly. These scholars share their approaches to fostering boundary-crossing by acknowledging minority voices and life experiences with respect and empathy.

Finally, there is also a theme on the boundary-crossing nature of interdisciplinarity. Bonnie Howe elaborates on the importance of metaphor and language in creating interdisciplinary spaces for teaching, learning, and dialoguing, while Ofelia Villero explains how quantitative and qualitative researchers should, and could, collaborate better despite methodological differences.

This book presents a way to cross boundaries, emphasizing empowerment of students and mutual learning between educators and learners. In this poetic action of boundary-crossing, the classroom becomes a safe space to quest one's own interior world while still critiquing the world, which can lead to participation in the effort to enhance justice in our diverse, multicultural world.

BIBLIOGRAPHY

Berling, Judith. *A Pilgrim in Chinese Culture: Negotiation Religious Diversity.* New York: Orbis Books, 2002.
———. *Understanding Other Religious Worlds: A Guide for Interreligious Education.* Maryknoll, NY: Orbis Books, 2004.

CHAPTER 2

Teaching and Learning Religion with Nones: An Application of Judith Berling's Pedagogy

Jung Eun Sophia Park

Abstract This chapter explores how Judith Berling's interreligious pedagogy can be applied to Nones, who do not have an affiliation with a particular religion yet manifest a desire for spirituality or religious wisdom. First, the author examines the literature on Nones in order to understand this group's spirituality and suggests an epistemology of other religions for Nones, comparing two different models, one a very much Western, Christian, or colonial model, and the other an engaging and encountering approach. The author then suggests a way of teaching at a university, which is centered on the students' desire for knowledge rather than on the educator's predetermined curriculum or teaching plans.

Keywords Nones · Gaze · Boundary crossings · Interreligious pedagogy · Teaching model · Epistemology · Mutual transformation

J. E. S. Park (✉)
Holy Names University, Oakland, CA, USA

© The Author(s) 2018
J. E. S. Park and E. S. Wu (eds.), *Interreligous Pedagogy*, Asian Christianity in the Diaspora, https://doi.org/10.1007/978-3-319-91506-7_2

When I began my undergraduate teaching in 2008 at Holy Names University, a Catholic liberal arts college in California, I was expected to teach the world religions courses, but I was not ready. My training assumed a scholarship and practice in theology, not necessarily in religious studies. It was a shift that required me to reach across the demarcating lines between Christianity and others, and it has impacted my understanding of religion in general and my Catholic faith in particular. Furthermore, this journey has prompted me to reconnect with my culturally embedded teaching of Eastern religions as a part of my spirituality. Almost every semester, I have taught this course with variations of course titles such as "World Religion Survey Course," "Eastern Religions," or "Abrahamic Religions." In this endeavor, I consider Christianity from a distance in order to teach it as the object of learning. Furthermore, I have noticed that my students do not seem to have as much interest in the subject matter as my colleagues with whom I share theological concerns and a vision in Christianity.

In this border crossing journey, Judith Berling's learning and teaching pedagogy has guided me. As Judith Berling claims, genuine teaching and learning includes going beyond the bounds, and, in so doing, she mentions that she often situated herself as the other or in the position of other. In *A Pilgrim in Chinese Culture*, Berling explains her own learning process, employing the concept of pilgrim, extending her vision and comprehension of herself through the study of Chinese religion and culture.[1] Berling, as an educator, a scholar, and a mentor to numerous students and scholars, remarks that she not only learned about Chinese culture, but also learned from it.[2] This phrase captures Judith Berling's spirit, which often manifests as an open attitude toward her teaching and learning, emphasizing self-implicated learning which leads into transformation.

Berling implemented engaging pedagogy, in which all participants, including herself, were supposed to learn through listening to one another with sincere respect, in her classroom at the Graduate Theological Union. The concept of respect in the learning context stems from one of the main Confucian virtues, the joy of seeking knowledge. *Analects*, an anthology of the words of Confucius, conveys the

---

[1] Judith Berling, *A Pilgrim in Chinese Culture: Negotiation Religious Diversity* (Maryknoll, NY: Orbis Books, 1997), 21.

[2] Ibid., 22.

philosophy of the sage, which is grounded in the joy of seeking knowledge. In the first chapter on learning (學而篇), the first passage reads, "學而時習之 不亦說乎?" If I translate this into English, the meaning would be "Isn't it a joy to be learning and often embody it?" The Chinese character "說" indicates more than simple joy; it is almost Zen-like bliss. This joy is embedded in Judith Berling's pedagogy, which includes learning, teaching, communicating, and practicing. In this spirit of joy, Berling's approach often emphasizes each student's personal interest, social location, and experience, de-emphasizing essentialism and negating universal and totalizing approaches. Very often in her class, the knowledge and questions each student brings are considered crucial, and she solidifies a common ground for seeking further knowledge in the classroom as a learning community.

Another phrase from *the Analects* which reminds me of Judith Berling's pedagogy reads, "三人行, 必有我師焉." This phrase can be translated as: "Wherever three people go, there must be one who can be my teacher." Judith's pedagogy focuses on the learning process, which does not necessarily separate students and teachers. Rather the classroom becomes a mutual learning space, and all participants share their insights and experiences freely. Judith often refers to bell hooks' engaged model as a way to liberate students. In hook's model, the educator is encouraged to embrace changes and to adapt the various ways of constructing knowledge in which students initiate the learning process.[3] This mutual learning makes students feel empowered and results in mutual transformation.

Reflecting on the two above passages from the Chinese text *Analects* in relation to Judith Berling's pedagogy, this approach can be summarized as a mutually transformative learning process in which students' interests and conditions are primary, and at this juncture, open dialogue and mutual respect between learners and educators are required. Accordingly, education should not be counted as transmission of knowledge but rather as a cultivation of students own inner resources.[4] Also, it

[3] bell hooks, *Teaching to Transgress: Education as the Practice of Freedom* (New York: Routledge, 1994), 44.

[4] Diana Chapman Walsh, "Transforming Education: An Overview," in *Education as Transformation: Religious Pluralism, Spirituality, and a New Vision for Higher Education in America*, ed. Victor H. Kazanjian, Jr. and Peter L. Laurence (New York: Peter Lang, 2013), 7.

would be fair to say that in education, learning and teaching cannot be separated but are interrelated as the two sides of a coin—companions in the journey to or pilgrimage of learning.

In the twenty-first century, the mode of knowing has evolved into various models, emphasizing the subjectivity of learners, and Judith Berling's scholarship on teaching and learning religion has been applied in various areas of interreligious studies, community service learning, and interdisciplinary studies, in emphasizing learning as boundary crossing. In this learning process, no one can occupy every part of knowledge, so collaboration is a primary requirement. Berling's scholarship and teaching creates a stepping stone to understanding other non-Christian religions, a way to deepen Christian understanding and learning from the other. As a fledgling professor of religious studies, I often remember her authentic excitement about her students' academic interests and their experiences as well as their critical analyses. Teaching religions in undergraduate classrooms based on Judith's learning and teaching pedagogy has enhanced the effectiveness of the learning process.

Now, my concern is how I can apply Berling's pedagogy to my students who identify themselves by stating, "I am not religious, but spiritual." With my gratitude to her scholarship of teaching and learning religion, which emphasizes dialogue and mutual understanding, I want to explore her educational approach regarding teaching my undergraduate students, most of whom belong to the category of None.

WHO ARE THE NONES?

In my religious studies classes, I often ask what each student's religion is. Most students say they are Catholics or Christians. However, if I ask how often they go to church or participate in any activity of the church, they say, "rarely." Thus, they actually fit in the category of Nones, those who do not have any religious affiliation or do not practice any religious faith. Today, one of the most popular themes in our society is being "spiritual, but not religious." In fact, this is even given the acronym SBNR. A significant and growing number of Americans are not identifying themselves as members of any religion. In other words, the biggest denomination in this country is the "Nones." According to a 2018 Pew Report, 27% of Americans—a quarter of the adult population—describe themselves as religiously unaffiliated. That's up from 16% just five years ago, and the percentage is higher among the young—up to 30% for those under the age of 30.[5] Who are these people who favor being spiritual over being institutionally religious? They are generally educated, liberal, and open-minded, with a deep sense of connection to the earth and a belief that there is more to life than the visible world. This "spiritual but not religious" group is the fastest-growing demographic in the USA. In the literature on Nones, a young author presents herself as the second generation of None.[6] Thus, we can project that a large percentage of college students belong to the group of None.

Recently, there has been research on the spirituality of Nones. Spiritual writer Thomas Moore suggests that in this multicultural and multi-religious society, a learner can borrow any wisdom, compassion, or method from various traditions and construct one's own religion.[7] For Moore, an individual's desire for meaning-making is a key component of the spirituality of Nones. Admittedly, there are many who follow such practices. I feel, nevertheless, skeptical about his approach for two reasons. First, he does not mention how the individual without any religious training constructs such knowledge or wisdom. He does not address accessibility to knowledge and seems to be under the assumption that everyone has resources and access to a certain knowledge base. Many fancy spiritual wisdoms are open to everyone simply through a credit card transaction. This way of shaping one's own religion could give rise to social justice issues in conjunction with spiritual capitalism or commercialism. Thus, people of fewer economic means may also lack spiritual capital.

Second, his approach raises an ethical question: is it appropriate to adapt any spiritual skill without commitment to or deep knowledge of the tradition? Many post-colonial scholars have warned that American-centered seeking, which does not pay attention to context and aims only

[5] Michael Lipka and Claire Gecewicz, "More Americans Now Say They Are Spiritual but Not Religious," *Pew Research Center* (September 6, 2017), accessed January 20, 2018, http://www.pewresearch.org/fact-tank/2017/09/06/more-americans-now-say-theyre-spiritual-but-not-religious/.

[6] Corinna Nicolaou, *A None's Story: Searching for Meaning Inside Christianity, Judaism, Buddhism and Islam* (New York: Columbia University Press, 2016), x.

[7] Thomas Moore, *A Religion of One's Own: A Guide to Creating a Personal Spirituality in a Secular World* (New York: Avery, 2014), 271.

at self-service, should be treated cautiously.[8] Religious teachings without comprehension of the sociohistorical and cultural context would be arbitrary, superficial, and shallow.

In *The Nones Are Alright*, Kaya Oakes shows through her extensive interviews among Nones that they still seek the meaning of life within and outside the Church, and reinvent community outside of church walls. Although this book pays more attention to Nones who were Catholics and those who turn to interfaith practice, she demonstrates that many young people seek meaning in their lives through the classroom and internet space, yearning for a community, and it is obvious that they do not appreciate the hierarchical- and cleric-centered structure of the Church.[9]

Another interesting work is *A None's Story* by Corinna Nicolaou. The author, as a second-generation None, explored major religions through visiting and engaging with people in their gatherings. She researched various sites and visited quite different styles of Christianity, as well as communities of Judaism, Buddhism, and Islam. In this journey, she observed and analyzed Christian gatherings and visited Jewish communities in L.A., where she spent her teen years with her many Jewish friends. In this place, her spiritual journey seemed to have meaning in that she was re-connected with her memories and her old friends. For Buddhism in the Bay Area, she went back to her college years of spiritual and mental darkness, and she appreciates the meditation that helped her face life during her college years. Also, she described an unexpected friendship with a Muslim woman. This book shows how she, as a None, gains information on religions and learns about them through engaging with people, deepening her sense of spiritual wisdom. Interestingly, her conclusion is to remain as a committed None whose spiritual practice would be self-guided.[10] This emphasizes that a None is not just someone lacking commitment to one specific religion, but perhaps rather one who has a commitment to aspects of various religions.

---

[8] See Donald Lopez, *Prisoners of Shangri-la: Tibetan Buddhism and the West* (Chicago, IL: University of Chicago Press, 1998), 11–12. The author critiques how Tibetan Buddhism is encapsulated by perception of the West.

[9] Kaya Oakes, *The Nones Are Alright: A New Generation of Believers, Seekers, and Those in Between* (Maryknoll, NY: Orbis Books, 2015), 197.

[10] Nicolau, *A None's Story*, 283.

In summary, this growing population of Nones does not have affiliation to a religion or a tradition yet seeks wisdom and spirituality through learning various religious traditions. Members of this group demonstrate a yearning for community, but that community could have various forms and it may not necessarily be a community within an institutionalized religion. Considering accessibility to and capability of gaining spiritual resources, it is crucial for Nones to learn how to access these wisdoms and to critique or interpret them. For the group of Nones, the classroom of world religions in a university would operate as a space for them to gain such access and skills. As a way to explore how to organize religion courses among the Nones, it would be helpful to examine the epistemology of other religions.

EPISTEMOLOGY OF OTHER RELIGIONS

In the 70s and 80s, the discourse of religious studies emphasized the religious *other*, or religious traditions different from Christianity, while critiquing any colonial way of constructing the *other*. In the 90s, the term interreligious education was coined, and many scholars emphasized the aspect of globalization and interreligious reality, paying attention to mutual transformation. This recognition raised an epistemological question regarding learning the other religions, namely how a learner constructs knowledge of *the other*.

Let me delineate three ways of constructing knowledge in terms of engaging with the *others*. The first model is a conventional one in which learners gain subjectivity through the *other*. Any religion or social group, as a unifying force which shapes a cohesive identity, is engaged in the othering process. In the Modern era, for example, the missionary movement functioned as a tool that elevated Western Christianity over any non-Christian faith.[11] During that era, the religious *other* was considered "primitive," "superstitious," and "underdeveloped," without comprehensive knowledge of the historical context or any possible deep meaning of the teachings of other religions. This gave rise to a moral problem of uncritically positioning the religious *other* as inferior, passive, and weak.[12]

[11] Edward Said, *Orientalism* (New York: Vintage Books, 1979), 42.

[12] Said, *Reflections on Exile and Other Essays* (Cambridge, MA: Harvard University Press), 301.

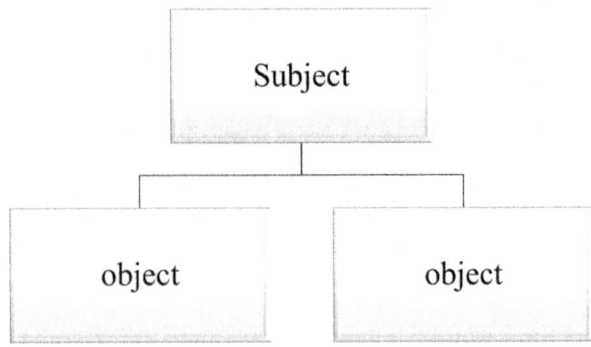

Fig. 2.1 Conventional model

However, this epistemology of *the other* still operates as an oppressive force toward people who do not practice *Western* Christianity. This approach has been criticized as a colonial model or an imperial model. The colonized or the sociopolitically oppressed's concept of self is shaped by the other and not by creating their own identity through comparing or contrasting with the *other*.[13] Unfortunately, many people around the globe still struggle to de-colonize their minds through re-learning their native religions and not by negating Christianity. For example, in Korea, liberation theologians studied Korean shamanism as a way to proclaim their own tradition and undo the Western missionary's *othering* process, and in so doing they tried to eliminate any internalized colonization (Fig. 2.1).

The second is the dialogical model, which admits the importance of mutual learning. If one takes the position of subject, the other takes the object, but more importantly, the other also takes the position of the subject simultaneously. In this model, dialogic partners possess their own critical self-knowledge of religion and of culture and commit to deepening their own knowledge from the *other*, understanding *the other* authentically through engagement. This model treats one's own religion as a critical tool for interpreting and understanding *the other*. As the Fig. 2.2 shows, one's own tradition or position, at least, is bigger than the other

---

[13] Jung Eun Sophia Park, *A Hermeneutic on Dislocation as Experience: Creating a Borderland, Constructing a Hybrid Identity* (New York: Peter Lang, 2011), 91.

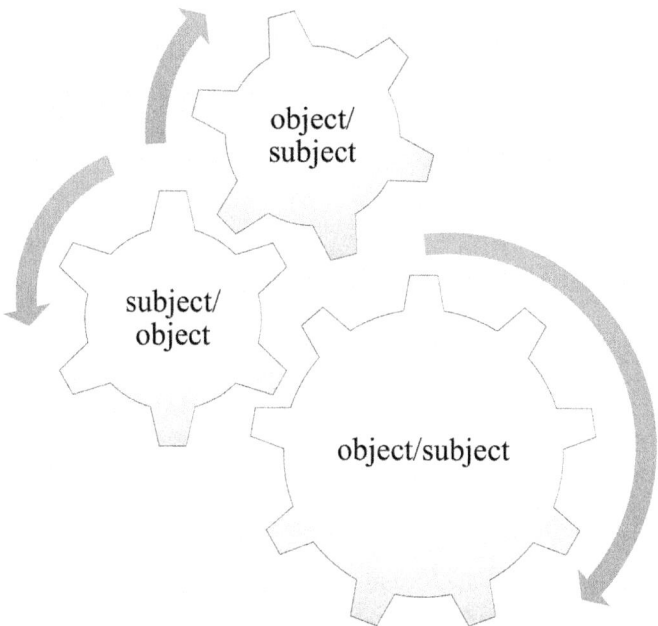

Fig. 2.2 Dialogical model

position or circle. De facto, Christianity still occupies a bigger space in terms of dialogue with other religions, and it indicates that one still sees through the lens of one's own tradition. I believe that Judith Berling's learning and teaching model belongs to the dialogical model. Her teaching theory and practice begin with the people of the Christian faith who want to explore other religions as a way to deepen their own religion as well as to extend their horizons. For this endeavor, the metaphor of a bridge would be employed.

The third model is the "empty subject" model. Here, a subject who is not situated within any organized religion does not feel obligated to defend the group or any particular religious tradition. Thus, the Nones' position-free stance in terms of lack of affiliation with any religion provides them with "hermeneutical privilege." In this model, subjects exist as free-floating agents with the various religions as objects to engage with. In this case, engagement takes the form of *gaze*, borrowing

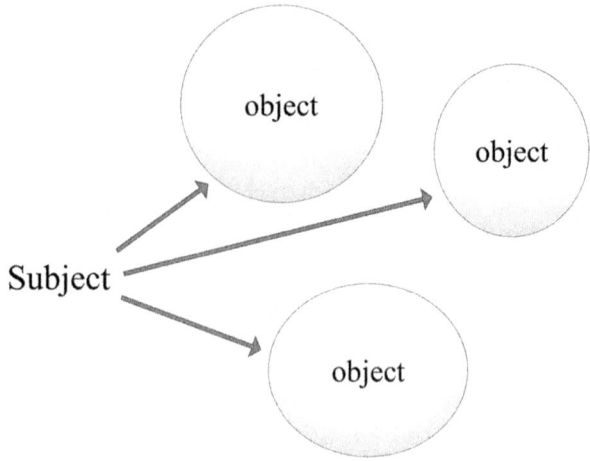

Fig. 2.3 Empty subject model

Jacque Lacan's term, which cannot be separated from and must be coupled with one's ego (Fig. 2.3).[14]

Jacque Lacan argues that any object that provokes a gaze brings a sense of strangeness,[15] as an unknown part of self. In his theory of psychology, something which invokes strangeness, fear, anxiety, or hatred is an unknown part of one's soul.[16] In the empty subject model, the subject gazes upon the objects as a projection of self and in this process, the subject gains self-knowledge. Thus, it is fair to say that the objects which would be engaged with the subject operate as stimuli to attain self-knowledge, which is a main element of spiritual knowledge.

When Jacque Lacan explains the concept of gaze, using the terms the object petit *a*, which indicates the object of desire, he uses the example

[14] Jacque Lacan, *The Seminar of Jacques Lacan, Book II, The Ego in Frued's Theory and in the Technique of Psychoanalysis, 1954–1955* (New York: W. W. Norton, 1991), 122.

[15] Jacque Lacan, *The Seminar of Jacques Lacan, Book XI: Four Fundamental Concepts of Psychoanalysis*, trans. Jacque-Alain Miller (New York: W. W. Norton, 1998), 75. Lacan further developed the concept of the object petit a as the object of desire which we seek in the other and which never resolved as surplus enjoyment.

[16] Julia Kristeva, *Strangers to Ourselves* (New York: Columbia University Press, 1991), 191–92.

of Chuang Tzu's dream. Chuang Tzu had a dream in which he became a butterfly, and after that, Chuang Tzu pondered whether he dreamed of being a butterfly or whether he is the butterfly who dreamed of being a Chuang Tzu. The butterfly in his dream is the object of gaze, and he later is conscious of what element of butterfly he saw. Thus, gaze is distinct from seeing and is controlled by context, culture, and environment and gives a glimpse how the one looks through the others. The object through gaze manifests a part of the subject that the one never fully sees.[17] Thus, to gaze upon an object(s) can be a way for one to attain knowledge of the subject.

In this multi-religious society, and if not attached to any position of religion or affiliated religions, the subject gazes on the object as a way to fill the lack inside the person. The gaze moves from a to b, to c, metonymically. A None who does not have any specific affiliation continuously gazes upon a religious or spiritual practice or community and may be intrigued by a certain aspect of teaching, prayer, or faith. In this case, gaze would include engaging, critiquing, and appreciating process. This process of gaze could challenge and nurture the person continuously, and it may confer comprehension of self-knowledge as well as the knowledge of the object from each of the various religious traditions. The position of the subject who does not have any affiliation can operate as a locus of privilege in seeking spiritual knowledge. This gaze model is distinct in that the subject does not have any fixed position and the subject gains a certain level of knowledge of self and of the object(s) through the gaze. Nones can learn religions through gaze which emphasizes one's own unsatisfied desire for infinity and wisdom. How this learning model can be actualized in the undergraduate class room requires consideration.

TEACHING RELIGIONS IN THE CLASSROOM

Keeping in mind the hunger for spiritual wisdom as well as the notion of the gaze of Nones, I will examine the learning outcomes of religious studies in higher education. Education researcher Barbara Walvoord argues that there is a "Great Divide" among faculty about how the learning space should be structured as a way to integrate spiritual

---

[17]Sinku Gazsike, *Lacan's Psychoanalysis: Object a is the Golden Number*, trans. Byoung Joon Kim from Japanese to Korean (Seoul: Eunhang Tree, 1995), 136.

development and critical thinking. Some faculty argue that course material itself should incorporate students' spiritual growth, while others contend that practices such as conversation and dialogues should be provided explicitly for spiritual growth.[18] The Religious Studies program of Holy Names University has learning outcomes congruent with university outcomes:

1. Practice communication skills needed for religious and philosophical discourse in a diverse world.
2. Critique moral and ethical norms that have shaped civilizations around the world in light of their religious and philosophical roots and utilize them to construct an adult conscience for personal and professional life.
3. Demonstrate personal growth, awareness, and skills of interpersonal, intercultural communication and understanding.
4. Apply critical thinking skills needed to evaluate past and present appropriations of religious tradition and experience.[19]

These four learning outcomes in my school emphasize critical thinking and communication skills rather than students' spiritual development. However, I often address a student's own spiritual development by requiring a learning outcome either that they are capable of interpreting a Bible passage according to their life contexts, or that they can create lists of their favorite spiritual teachings, which integrate various religious learnings into their spiritual practice. Religious studies courses, employing Judith Berling's pedagogy, help them to cooperate with learning outcomes for spiritual development, emphasizing self-knowledge.

POSSIBLE NEW TEACHING MODEL

Judith Berling's mutual learning pedagogy will be utilized, emphasizing listening practice and mutual engagement as a new teaching model. I set six steps to follow which can be employed in any classroom for the Nones. The first step is to create a safe environment by establishing a

---

[18] Barbara E. Walvoored, *Teaching and Learning in College Introductory Religion Courses* (New York: Blackwell, 2008), 94.

[19] *Holy Names University 2017–2018 Catalog*, 79.

sense of community. Faculty should pay attention to creating a learning community in which no student will feel excluded. Students who do not have much religious practice or any specific faith often do not feel comfortable in the Religious Studies classes. Faculty needs to invite students to express freely what they think. In this environment, the whole class would collect the prior knowledge through which students would bring their own experience. Each student would initially interpret any given practice or concept in approximation. For example, if the word "grace" is brought up during the dialogue, each student, for understanding, needs to translate it into their own language, which appropriates their sensibility.[20] In this border crossing journey, Judith Berling's learning and teaching approach which aims to empower students has guided me. Because Nones are not trained in a religious tradition, this would be a crucial process that would give students confidence.

The second step is to draw a conceptual map. Faculty should provide possible categories such as worship, basic teaching, meditation, ritual, cosmology, anthropology, and social engagement. All materials would be allocated according to these categories. For example, a student can speak of one experience of being invited to a Bar Mitzvah, which would be located under the category of ritual. Or a student can share a mindfulness practice to be placed under the category of meditation. A student might also offer something without a formal name such as simply a description. The experience can bring into the classroom a vivid description of color, odor, or voice that students have experienced before.

The third step is to visit sites. Usually, I have assigned a visiting project as a final synthesis. However, after considering the condition of a student who does not have any hands-on experience of religion and Berling's pedagogy of engagement, I have decided to locate this portion as a central piece of the class learning process. The first visit would be communal in terms of preparation, on-site visitation, and synthesis. The preparation includes contacting the religious site and making a list of questions. Once the site visit is arranged, all students read their Web site and prepare what is required for the visit. After the visit, each student describes their experience. In one class, we visited a Zen Buddhist temple near Muir Woods park. After the visit, we discussed what Zen Buddhism

---

[20] Sandra Schneiders, "A Hermeneutical Approach to the Study of Christian Spirituality," *Christian Spirituality Bulletin* (Spring 1994): 9–14.

is, focusing on its practice in the Bay Area. On this visit, many students expressed the desire to revisit and have a longer conversation with an American monk, who was a taxi driver in San Francisco.

After this practice visit, each student decided to visit a religious site of their choosing. They made four groups and visited at least twice and made careful and complete descriptions using the categories that we set up.

The fourth step is to analyze the extensive descriptions. In this step, teaching materials are rearranged according to students' interest. In the class that I mentioned in the third step, I focused on Buddhism and Hinduism, emphasizing the difference and unique characteristics of various sects of two Eastern religions. Students brought films and video clips that conveyed the teachings of these religions.

The fifth step is to introduce some theories of post-colonialism and feminist theory. However, the choice of these topics is based on the students' questions and inquires. Students raised questions about gender equality in relation to race and ethnicity. For example, when they visited a Buddhist temple, White American women took a leadership role while Asian members, including monks, seemed passive. Given that circumstance, we explored the post-colonial relationships of Eastern religions, and for that purpose, I provided pertinent articles for discussion.

For the final step, students share impressive learning that they want to adapt as their life principle or personal spirituality. In this process, the whole class shares new knowledge and celebrates the intellectual and spiritual growth together as a learning community, creating a ritual gratitude circle. In this ritual, all students acknowledge one another the insights or knowledge gained through the mutual engagement.

CLOSING REMARKS

Berling's pedagogy, which can be characterized as mutual and engaging teaching and learning, empowers students and transforms educators as well as students. Berling's pedagogy can be applied especially for Nones, who are a rapidly growing population in the USA. In this journey in the terrain of border crossing, the classroom will be a space where one's own assumptions are challenged, and as a result, all participants, including the educator, will enhance their understanding.

In Berling's pedagogy, as in Chuang Tsu's dream, the subject freely moves into the position of object, and this flexibility and openness can guide students to actively engage with various spiritual wisdoms. In this safe learning space, Nones can bring a more critical perspective while at the same time learn how to access and dialogue with people of various spiritual and religious traditions. This intellectual curiosity and desire for the other brings a deep self-knowledge. In my dream or hope, I see myself as a butterfly that touches diverse flowers with many other butterflies and in so doing helps flowers to spread their life force. From each flower, I gain honey, the spiritual wisdom.

BIBLIOGRAPHY

Berling, Judith. *A Pilgrim in Chinese Culture: Negotiation Religious Diversity.* Maryknoll, NY: Orbis Books, 1997.

———. *Understanding Other Religious Worlds: A Guide for Interreligious Education.* Maryknoll, NY: Orbis Books, 2004.

Holy Names University 2017–2018 Catalog.

hooks, bell. *Teaching to Transgress: Education as the Practice of Freedom.* New York: Routledge, 1994.

Jacques, Lacan. *The Seminar of Jacques Lacan, Book II: The Ego in Freud's Theory and in the Technique of Psychoanalysis.* Translated by Jacque-Alain Miller. New York: W. W. Norton, 1991.

———. *The Seminar of Jacques Lacan, Book XI: Four Fundamental Concepts of Psychoanalysis.* Translated by Jacque-Alain Miller. New York: W. W. Norton, 1998.

Kristeva, Julia. *Strangers to Ourselves*, 191–92. New York: Columbia University Press, 1991.

Lipka, Michael, and Claire Gecewicz. "More Americans Now Say Ther're Spiritual but Not Religious." *Pew Research Center* (September 6, 2017). Accessed January 20, 2018. http://www.pewresearch.org/fact-tank/2017/09/06/more-americans-now-say-theyre-spiritual-but-not-religious/.

Lopez, Donald. *Prisoners of Shangri-la: Tibetan Buddhism and the West.* Chicago, IL: University of Chicago Press, 1998.

Moore, Thomas. *A Religion of One's Own: A Guide to Creating a Personal Spirituality in a Secular World.* New York: Avery, 2014.

Nicolaou, Corinna. *A None's Story: Searching for Meaning Inside Christianity, Judaism, Buddhism and Islam.* New York: Columbia University Press, 2016.

Oakes, Kaya. *The Nones Are Alright: A New Generation of Believers, Seekers, and Those in Between.* Maryknoll, NY: Orbis Books, 2015.

Park, Jung Eun Sophia. *A Hermeneutic on Dislocation as Experience: Creating a Borderland, Constructing a Hybrid Identity.* New York: Peter Lang, 2011.

Said, Edward. *Orientalism.* New York: Vintage Book, 1979.

————. *Reflections on Exile and Other Essays*. Cambridge, MA: Harvard University Press, 2000.

Schneiders, Sandra. "A Hermeneutical Approach to the Study of Christian Spirituality." *Christian Spirituality Bulletin* (Spring 1994): 9–14.

Sinku, Gazsike. *Lacan's Psychoanalysis: Object a is the Golden Number*. Translated by Byoung Joon Kim from Japanese to Korean. Seoul: Eunhang Tree, 1995.

Walsh, Diana Chapman. "Transforming Education: An Overview." In *Education as Transformation: Religious Pluralism, Spirituality, and a New Vision for Higher Education in America*, edited by Victor H. Kazanjian, Jr. and Peter L. Laurence. New York: Peter Lang, 2013.

Walvoored, Barbara E. *Teaching and Learning in College Introductory Religion Courses*. New York: Blackwell, 2008.

CHAPTER 3

Crossing Disciplines: Beyond Religious Studies and the Health Sciences

Ofelia O. Villero

Abstract In this chapter, the author narrates her personal story of how Judith Berling's model of teaching and learning helped her cross disciplines from religious studies to health sciences at a time when the Humanities (under which religious studies is classified) are under siege. It also gives an example from the author's professional life as a community-based participatory health researcher on how Berling's conceptualization of the learning process can be applied equally to a non-religious context as in the author's qualitative participatory action research project. The author concludes that Berling's mentorship and articulation of the learning process make it possible to "enter other worlds through engaging and crossing boundaries of significant difference" and, along the way, develop one's own voice and that of others.

Keywords Community-based participatory research · Qualitative research · Philippine culture · Empathy · Humanities

O. O. Villero (✉)
University of California, San Francisco, San Francisco, CA, USA

© The Author(s) 2018   25
J. E. S. Park and E. S. Wu (eds.), *Interreligous Pedagogy*, Asian Christianity in the Diaspora, https://doi.org/10.1007/978-3-319-91506-7_3

In her book, *Understanding Other Religious Worlds*, Judith Berling narrates an incident where, as a college freshman taking a course in Protestantism, Catholicism, and Judaism in the USA, she had to answer a question on a final examination regarding the major provisions of civil rights legislation pending in Congress. The question was, "Based on what you have learned, what *should be* the positions of these religious groups on this legislation?" She thought that the question was challenging, but saw it also as bringing "the learning down to issues shaping lives in the contemporary context." Linking that earlier insight to the contemporary teaching and learning of religions, Berling states, "We too often teach and learn other religions as though they do not have an impact on our actual lives."[1]

I share her sentiment—which I feel applies to other fields as well—that we teach and learn as though our actions were impersonal and objective and that we are teaching and learning only data. However, models of teaching and learning greatly shape our attitudes, ideas, behavior, vision of the future, daily interactions, and relationships. I know, for I speak from experience. Her model of teaching and learning, as she lived it as my graduate studies teacher and mentor, enabled me to cross disciplines from religious studies to health sciences research and helped frame my daily work as a qualitative/Community-Based Participatory Researcher. Although my story is not strictly about interreligious education, it nevertheless proves the organic and profound influences of a teaching and learning model that aims, as articulated by Berling, Maxine Green, and bell hooks, to "give learners voice and the ability to listen, to establish networks of relationships, to build bridges, and to live and move effectively in the world."[2] Therefore, it is important for me to look back and relate my story in a deeply personal way instead of treating it as one more byte in an ocean of "big data."[3]

Crossing disciplines is never easy, but in the current climate where the humanities—under which religious studies is classified—are under siege,[4,5] it is even more difficult. The emphasis of education and political

---

[1] Judith A. Berling, *Understanding Other Religious Worlds: A Guide to Interreligious Education* (New York: Maryknoll, 2004), 79.

[2] Ibid., 80.

[3] For purposes of this paper, "big data" refers to digital data collected in a massive scale, which are unstructured and require data analytics to determine their value.

[4] Michael Brown, "The Sciences vs. The Humanities, a Power Struggle," *Chronicle of Higher Education*, April 11, 2011.

[5] Tamara Lewin, "As Interest Fades in the Humanities, Colleges Worry," *New York Times*, October 30, 2013.

leaders on a core curriculum based on science, technology, engineering, and mathematics (STEM) and the decline in funding and student enrollment in the humanities have undermined the importance of a humanities background and lowered regard for people with majors in the field.[6] In the health sciences, the rise of evidence-based practice as a paradigm and methodology for health care has called into question the utility of qualitative research,[7] under which Community-Based Participatory Research falls. These trends have exacerbated the traditional view of religion as a public-health problem, based on published cases suggesting that being religiously observant may pose specific health risks (e.g., impact of fasting during Ramadan for observant Muslims with diabetes) and the belief of many health care professionals that religiously based traditions may impede the growth of modernity (e.g., the debate on Islam and modernity) and that religious convictions may obstruct the implementation of biomedical health care delivery (e.g., the controversy regarding immorality and the slow response to HIV).[8]

In my experience, crossing over from religious studies to health sciences is the same as learning another religion. As Berling observes about the process of learning another religion, it involves "enter[ing] other worlds through engaging and crossing boundaries of significant difference."[9] The most obvious difference is the health sciences' reliance and emphasis on quantitative research, which is the use of numerical data as the unit of analysis.[10] However, since I work as a qualitative/Community-Based Participatory Researcher, I normally do not deal with statistical analysis. Nevertheless, due to the entrenchment of evidence-based practice in health care, qualitative research has increasingly taken on a utilitarian function, by turning theories into "material and measurable use in practice" such as clinical assessment guides and appraisal tools that "have greater psychometric and cultural specificity and sensitivity"[11] and

---

[6] Ibid.

[7] Margarete Sandelowski, "Using Qualitative Research," *Qualitative Health Research* 14, no. 10 (2004), http://doi.org/10.1177/1049732304269672.

[8] Linda L. Barnes, "New Geographies of Religion and Healing: States of the Field," *Practical Matters Journal*, March 1, 2011, https://np.me/p6QAmj-7G.

[9] Berling, Understanding Other Religious Worlds, 64.

[10] Melanie Birks and Jane Mills, *Grounded Theory: A Practical Guide* (London: Sage, 2011), 146.

[11] Sandelowski, "Using Qualitative Research," 1372.

by clarifying, explaining, and verifying the instrumental value or clinical significance of quantitative research findings.[12] In other words, qualitative research must demonstrate its usability and usefulness in everyday health care practice. For the most part, religious studies has escaped the pressure and consequences of evidence-based practice. In crossing disciplines, I have found that I owe much to Judith Berling's model of handling difference, which she generated at the juncture of her own areas of research: learning theory, the study of religions, and theological learning.

Although it had never entered my mind to cross disciplines in my professional life, I was always interested in pursuing a research career rather than teaching. I first articulated this interest in Judith's class on Interdisciplinarity, which helped students design a course and create a course syllabus, focus on problems that aspiring higher-education teachers inevitably face in the classroom, and formulate plans for colleges and universities to target for teaching employment. The course grounded doctoral students in the realities of a teaching career, but, most importantly, it identified and encouraged the internalization of pedagogies that would elevate the teaching and learning process into a lifelong path of spiritual and intellectual growth.

While I knew that the normal goal in pursuing a doctorate in religious studies is a teaching career, I was nevertheless attracted to research as a full-time job after graduation. The problem was that there were hardly any paid positions for conducting research on religions on a full-time basis. When Judith asked us, one by one, to articulate our vision of where we wanted to be after degree conferment, I said I saw myself doing research on women and religion rather than teaching. I was the only one in the class who had a research goal in mind, and as a Filipino immigrant with a community-oriented culture, I felt a bit isolated and embarrassed in my aloneness. But Judith took my vision seriously, and instead of sounding perplexed, skeptical, or, heaven forbid, scornful, she honored my vision by responding that perhaps religious studies departments should broaden their course offerings to serve students like me who were more interested in pursuing a non-teaching career but who would nevertheless benefit from a doctoral program that skewed toward research. That interchange not only gave me confidence to pursue my vision but also hinted at the underlying teaching and learning process that Judith articulated and embodied.

[12] Ibid., 1373.

As a doctoral student at the Graduate Theological Union, it took me a while to get comfortable with Judith Berling. Judith's academic specialization was Chinese religions, and therefore, I assumed that, being a Protestant and not Chinese, she was a textbook scholar relying on ancient texts for her expertise, whereas I aspired to become a post-colonial scholar of religion who would be dealing with contemporary issues.

From my narrow and provincial perspective, this meant that she was tainted with orientalism, which Edward Said defines in his book of the same title as a discourse that presumes the superiority of the West, and thus the inferiority of the East, and was instrumental in advancing the imperial designs of the European powers and the USA as well as nurturing the West's sense of privilege.[13] I did not know then that Judith's model of teaching was an antidote to Said's rightful criticism of the construction of "otherness." In fact, in her book, she describes orientalism as:

> also a form of mastery because the Western orientalist scholar presumes to speak for the other, who remains voiceless and disenfranchised, and the Western student believes that the Western scholar's interpretation gives one a coherent grasp of (hold on) the other. The colonialist and orientalist scholars rely on ancient texts in their libraries believed to capture the early (and thus "true") teachings of the religion; they do not offer their armchair reconstructions for correction by the living adherents of religions.[14]

My discomfort with Judith vanished and was replaced with respect and affection when circumstances brought me under her mentorship as I finished my doctoral studies. Judith's way of being an educator involves—in the words of bell hooks—providing the "necessary conditions where learning can most deeply and intimately begin."[15] In my case, a lesson in openness and inclusion from Judith did not happen in a lecture hall as we shared information on a religious text or ritual but occurred when she made me aware that a "shared commitment and a common good binds us."[16] We were united in a desire for intellectual growth, a search for knowledge, which for me was also a journey of personal freedom.

---

[13] Edward W. Said, *Orientalism* (New York: Random House, Inc., 1979).

[14] Berling, *Understanding Other Religious Worlds*, 43.

[15] Ibid., 24.

[16] Ibid., 25.

As articulated by hooks in her concept of engaged pedagogy, learning flourishes when there is a sense of community, where each member—teacher or student—engages the other to arrive at a common understanding of our connection to each other. She writes: "What we all ideally share is the desire to learn—to receive actively knowledge that enhances our intellectual development and our capacity to live more fully in the world."[17] Such a learning process results in the learner's empowerment and the development of voice and agency.

At the time, within the community of fellow graduate students, I felt that my location, the starting point of my journey, set me apart from everybody else. These differences created the unease that sometimes made me feel helpless and reticent. Not only was I the first person in my family to go to college and on to a doctoral program—which was enough to create tension from the pressure of expectations—but my youth also took place in impoverished conditions and under political persecution. Residing in a violent neighborhood, I was also witness to brutality, particularly against women. Someone had to acknowledge my difference to be able to reach me. When Judith offered to be my advisor without demanding that I "jump through hoops," she breached an invisible barrier. Although it may have been unconscious on her part, I interpreted her action as a gesture of empathy. Born and raised in the Philippines with a culture that thrives on empathy, I responded positively to what I viewed as empathetic signs.

Judith calls the ideal of empathy, which she defines as "looking with the eyes of another," problematic when applied to the study of religions, "for it severely underestimates the challenge of understanding across lines of difference." She writes:

> In place of sympathy or empathy, seeing *myself* in the other – and thus still looking through my own cultural and experiential lenses – it is important to attend to the particular words, images, and behaviors through which the other represents himself. How is meaning expressed, lived out, understood, and articulated in the context I am seeing to understand? Attending to the particular words, images, and behaviors important in the other context helps me to acknowledge the particularity, the difference, of the religion I am trying to understand.[18]

---

[17] bell hooks, *Teaching to Transgress: Education as the Practice of Freedom* (New York: Routledge, 1994), 39–40.

[18] Ibid., 39.

Despite her objection, Judith does not completely reject empathy as a means to understand difference. She demands a carefully nuanced approach to empathy, which can be found in Maxine Greene's concept of imagination, from her book *Releasing the Imagination: Essays on Education, the Arts and Social Change.* Greene states that imagination is what makes empathy possible.

> It [imagination] is what enables us to cross the empty spaces between ourselves and those we teachers have called "other" over the years. If those others are willing to give us clues, we can look in some manner through the strangers' eyes and hear through their ears. That is because, of all our cognitive capacities, imagination is the one that permits us to give credence to alternative realities. It allows us to break with the taken for granted, to set aside familiar distinctions and definitions.[19]

Judith points out that Greene's approach is noteworthy because it pays close attention to the clues from others and admits that the imaginative grasp will always be partial, as evidenced by the phrase "in some manner." Instead of looking at similarities, which could very well be superficial, Greene's process focuses on the differences to understand the subject. Judith explains:

> As the scholar attends to the distinctive languages, patterns, and behavior in the context, she gradually sees or hears how these characteristics are given meaning in that context. The distinctive language or behaviors become the "handles" around which understanding begins to emerge. The difference of foreignness of the language or behavior underscores the challenge of understanding, the gap between the learner's prior experience and this religious other. Attending to the differences, the gap, illustrates what needs to be learned; it challenges the learner to grapple with new words, behaviors, and meanings until some degree of understanding begins to emerge. …This requires attention to and respect for difference.[20]

As an "other" in real life here in the USA most of the time, I interpret Judith's statement as a way for a learner/viewer to see me as I am and refrain from making judgments and assumptions about who or what I

---

[19] Maxine Greene, *Releasing the Imagination: Essays on Education, the Arts, and Social Change* (San Francisco: Jossey-Bass, 1995), 3.

[20] Berling, *Understanding Other Religious Worlds*, 40.

am based on her location and set of experiences. The process becomes an exercise of freedom for both the "other" and the learner/viewer and is empowering.

As I learned to trust and develop my own voice under Judith's mentorship, I also became interested in a branch of qualitative research and Community-Based Participatory Research or CBPR. An alternative to traditional research approaches that "assume a phenomenon may be separated from its context for purposes of study,"[21] CBPR instead partners with community members, organizational representatives, and researchers in all phases of a research project to include the social, physical, and structural environment of subjects in the study. It aims to use the gathered expertise to "enhance understanding of a given phenomenon and integrate the knowledge gained with action to benefit the community involved."[22] By allowing community input into a project, CBPR enables the "innovative adaptation of existing resources, explores local knowledge and perceptions, and empowers people by considering them agents who can investigate their situations."[23] Through an emphasis on collaborative effort, it provides a platform that can bridge cultural differences among participants and break down the lack of trust communities may have in relation to research. The participation of the community to effect change makes CBPR a model for reducing health disparities in vulnerable populations, such as ethnic minorities and the elderly.

The key to evaluating participatory action research is the "extent to which identified problems was resolved and the extent to which oppressive structures were undermined and emancipatory goals were achieved."[24] Thus to succeed, CBPR must give voice to the voiceless, representing and interpreting their stories to help them understand themselves and their context vis-à-vis a health problem. It must also point to ways in which research findings can be used to satisfy the community's health objectives. In other words, CBPR seeks to empower marginalized communities to understand their problems, offer their own solutions, and find ways to implement those solutions. For this reason,

---

[21] Patricia A. Holkup et al., "Community-Based Participatory Research: An Approach to Intervention Research with a Native American Community," *ANS Advances in Nursing Science* 27, no. 3 (2004): 163.

[22] Ibid.

[23] Ibid., 164.

[24] Sandelowski, "Using Qualitative Research," 1371.

I have found Berling's interpretation of the learning process helpful in framing and understanding my CBPR work.

In Chapter 5 of *Understanding Other Religious Worlds*, Judith focuses on the process of learning another religion. However, I feel that her interpretation is equally applicable in other fields, and thus, in outlining her five stages of the learning process, I took the liberty of deleting references to learning another religion. She condenses the process into five threads, namely: (1) encountering difference/entering other worlds; (2) initial response from one's own location; (3) conversation and dialogue; (4) developing relationships/living one's own understanding; and (5) internalizing the process.[25] Judith qualifies that the stages do not always follow in sequence and the various aspects of learning reinforce one another.

In CBPR as in learning another religion, the steps in the process do not always occur in linear progression. Sometimes they happen simultaneously, overlap, or occur in reverse. However, characteristics of every step can be identified and remain consistent throughout the process. The essence of CBPR is community partnership. Thus, all research projects involve various partners with a stake in the outcomes of the research. Instead of one world, I encounter many worlds simultaneously because community partners and research colleagues come from different locations, not only geographically but also educationally, socially, economically, and even politically. Yet we all subscribe to the idea that the aim of the research is to correct a health disparity by improving the health outcomes of a vulnerable population.

As described by Berling, the first principle in encountering difference is to recognize and acknowledge it, not to reduce another person, culture, or religion to a variation of what the viewer knows based on her own experiences and practices.[26] In recognizing difference, I have learned that my response to it requires flexibility and is dependent on the location and action of the person I am encountering. As an example, I relate an incident that occurred between me and a principal quantitative investigator just learning the ropes of CBPR research. As the person who acquired funding for the research project, the principal investigator is considered the head of the research team.

---

[25] Berling, *Understanding Other Religious Worlds*, 65–80.
[26] Ibid., 66.

For this research project involving low-income older adults or seniors with diabetes and cardiovascular disease, the principal investigator instructed junior researchers from a community-based organization to observe study participants as if they were viewing "animals in a zoo," as objectively and impersonally as possible. With my religious studies background and as a qualitative researcher with years of experience in CBPR, I balked at her idea and protested to her supervisor, who explained that it was her background in quantitative research that led to her unwitting statement. In my subsequent encounter with this principal investigator, I advised her to take a cultural sensitivity training course to advance the goals of the project. While she took my advice, her continued antagonism resulted in my departure from the project. However, she was able to rectify her initial blunder and has become a seasoned qualitative researcher.

Examples from my initial breast cancer research project illustrate the rest of the stages of Judith's learning model. The goal of this project was to answer the central question, "What support model is culturally meaningful and sustainable for Filipinos with experience of breast cancer?" Cancer statistics showed that Filipino women had a higher rate of mortality from breast cancer than other ethnic groups. To correct this health disparity, it was crucial that Filipinos diagnosed with breast cancer gain access to health care at the earliest stages of the disease. Before proposing a solution and securing funding from the government and health care organizations, the project needed to figure out which support model would be effective in the long run in decreasing Filipino deaths from breast cancer. To do this, we needed the patients to tell us what elements—cultural, physical, spiritual, mental—were crucial in building and sustaining an infrastructure that would make an impact in their lives. I had to recruit low-income, low-English-proficient immigrant women with breast cancer, who were uninsured or underinsured to be part of the study. It was their voices that would make any intervention successful.

For the second stage of the learning process, Berling states, "Learners must start from the language they know in order to find a way into the language they will need to understand another community."[27] As a researcher, I used participant observation and in-depth interviews to understand the world of my Filipino human subjects. I attended Filipino cultural events, spent time in conversation in women's homes and with their families, and accompanied them to oncology appointments and cancer-support group meetings. Yet my presence in their lives was not enough to encourage them to give voice to their feelings about breast cancer and articulate their ideas about how to help themselves. I needed a group of women who would be willing to spend time with me, at least two hours a month, to share their experiences, go over my field notes, and "interpret" with me the findings in order to identify the crucial factors that would constitute a health intervention for patients like them. I turned to the Filipino concept of empathy to close the gap separating me from the women. The concept allowed me to use the language of my study participants to enter their world.

Relationship building, or *pakikisama* in Tagalog, is an important core cultural value that frames how Filipinos understand and interpret their experiences, including their dealings with health care providers and professionals. According to Filipino social scientists Maggay and Aleto,[28,29] *pakikisama* initiates the building of relationships by making the other feel welcome, safe, and nurtured. It is particularly helpful in a situation in which people who are thrown together come from different social backgrounds, positions, ethnicities, and races. *Pakikisama* can act as an equalizer, paving the way for dialogue involving participants who are open, speak freely, and learn from each other.

A process in itself, *pakikisama* pivots around the custom called "feeling out," which is the primary use of intuitive and affective faculties to assess an individual or a situation, instead of relying on cognitive behavior such as asking a direct question to acquire the knowledge one needs. It involves the reading of indirect verbal and non-verbal cues such as tone of voice, facial expressions, and hand gestures, as well as caring acts like offering food to strangers, to determine not so much what is being communicated but the kind of person who is doing the communicating. Philippine culture, which is highly relational, attaches a great deal of value to personal relations and associations, which can serve as

[28] Melba P. Maggay, *Pahiwatig: Kagawiang Pangkomunikasyon ng Pilipino* [Intimations: Habitual Filipino Modes of Communications] (Quezon City, Philippines: Ateneo de Manila University Press, 2002).

[29] Alberto E. Alejo, *Tao Po! Tuloy Po!* [It's a Person! Please Come In!] (Quezon City, Philippines: Ateneo de Manila University Press, 1990).

the context for information or educational content to stand out and be heard, and then acted upon. It is not so much the message found in brochures, flyers, or even educational workshops that can induce an attitude or behavioral change in individuals, but a messenger who is perceived as caring and trustworthy.

The research team members used this understanding of *pakikisama* to recruit women to a Community Advisory Board (CAB). Membership recruitment to the CAB posed problems because of the unavailability of potential members. The candidate pool consisted of low-income women, single mothers, or heads of households who needed to hold down two jobs or more and work long hours to support themselves and family members in the USA as well as those whom they left behind in the Philippines. Carving time from their fatiguing schedules to attend several meetings, even only once a month, would entail sacrifices on the women's part. The research team knew several women who fit all the criteria except for availability and would have been tremendous assets for the CAB. However, asking them to become CAB members regardless of their life situation would have, in a sense, put them on the spot. It would signal that the team was considering our own goals above their situation and interests.

At this point, the third stage in Berling's learning process—conversation and dialogue—is relevant. She states that "both parties to such conversations must be mutually respectful and attentive to the voice of the other, always wary of superficial or easy agreement. They have to be willing to listen and to learn and understand the distinctive language in which the dialogue partner expresses herself. Such listening may enable the partner to move forward."[30]

Pakikisama obligated the team to not embarrass the women, who were our recruitment targets, by putting them in a position to turn down our request, which would have led to tension between them and us. Instead, we had to make our request indirectly, either through an intermediary or by broaching the subject of CAB membership without referring directly to their participation. If potential candidates felt that they were interested in becoming CAB members and could fulfill the requirements, then it was up to them to say so, with no perceptible pressure nor any expectation from us. When they came to a decision, either for

[30] Berling, *Understanding Other Religious Worlds*, 74.

or against participation, we supported it enthusiastically. Through this recruitment process, six women agreed to become CAB members. The next step after recruitment was for the new members to be comfortable with each other and cohere as a group.

While we had developed good relations with each individual CAB member, the women themselves were strangers to each other. For them to be comfortable working together, they had to cohere as a group through *pakikisama*. A commonality—breast cancer experience—did not automatically anchor the group and, in fact, was problematic. Although immersed in the community, most of the CAB members had not publicly admitted having breast cancer, due to their awareness of the stigmatization and the gossip that could follow. In writing about the impact of gossip on the Filipino psyche, historian Rafael states that "gossip produces the opposite effect of pity: suspicion, disrespect, disbelief."[31] It was fear for their privacy and becoming a target of gossip that kept some women from attending support groups in the first place. It was necessary, therefore, for the women to "feel out" the other members of the advisory board in order to trust them.

The fourth stage of the learning process—developing relationships/ living one's own understanding—took place when the women CAB members started meeting on a regular basis. Berling describes this stage as providing the "basis for new relationships and for transformative actions and the understanding and linguistic flexibility to work with others who bring very different life practices and views to any common cause."[32]

The CAB's first meeting was mainly devoted to socializing. Over food, we introduced individual members to each other, bringing out informal, personal connections from our own knowledge of the women. The next meeting heightened their comfort level with each other after a presentation of our partial research findings, which included actual statements from interviewees about the meaning and impact of breast cancer on their lives. After the presentation, members shared their personal and intimate struggles with the disease, forging a deeper and caring relationship with each other. By the third meeting, members started to grapple

---

[31] Vicente Rafael, "Your Grief Is Our Gossip: Overseas Filipinos and Other Spectral Presences," *Public Culture* 9, no. 2 (1997): 289.

[32] Berling, *Understanding Other Religious Worlds*, 79.

with developing a support model, and at the last session, after intense yet amiable discussions, they came up with a culturally meaningful concept of support, *buong puso* or whole heart, as a framework for a sustainable support model for Filipinos.

The *buong puso* framework, as conceptualized by the CAB, consisted of the following:

- **Breast cancer services that target the whole person.** A CAB member explained, "I was thinking about something that can help the woman as a whole – the woman as mother, as sister, as daughter, in dealing with the illness." In agreeing with her, the group clarified that the patient or survivor continues with her familial roles from cancer diagnosis, through treatment and recovery, and services must include other family members, particularly the children.
- **"One-stop shopping" or interconnected, holistic services.** They described their experience of being sent from one facility to another, from one social service agency to another as fragmentary, a discontinuity that left them confused and vulnerable. A member related: "A navigator or case manager tells me to go here, to go there, do this, do that. But what I really need and want at the moment is one person or one place I can go to [for my needs].... I don't have to go to [another place] and talk to someone else and start all over again." A second member concurred: "Yeah, one place. Like if you are in this facility, it should be linked to the hospital and the pharmacy. You know, interconnected. One whole."
- **In the context of Filipino culture, services that do not just "help" but "support."** The group imagined services that would be provided wholeheartedly, that "penetrated deeply" into the heart. One member distinguished "help" from "support" with the definition: "To me, 'help' means 'doing something for someone' but 'support' means 'walking side by side' with that person." Another member pointed out: "*Buong puso* already includes assistance, but it means more than that. It includes the idea of becoming bosom buddies, mentoring someone who is just beginning. Also, bonding.... It's all support coming from your whole heart."

According to the CAB, support, if given in the framework of *buong puso*, became relational, providing not just help through temporary financial relief, continuing health education, and diversion through knitting classes, but a deep human connection in spite of differences that exist between the ill and the healthy, between those who can afford health care and those who cannot, between the rich and the poor, and even between institutions and individuals.

From a CBPR perspective, the project was successful because the women came up with a culturally meaningful and sustainable model that had practical implications in addressing health disparities in an underserved community. To this day, the participants in the CAB are independently running a support group for women with experience of breast cancer and senior or older adults in San Francisco. It does not have funding from any government agency, private, or non-governmental organizations. The group has become self-sustaining and meets every Monday for lunch, goes on field trips, hosts health-information lectures, cultural events, and other activities that can benefit the community.

The result proves the fifth stage of Berling's model, internalizing the process. As Judith clarifies, internalization of the learning process is "not a process for absorbing information but as empowerment of learners to engage broader and broader spheres of knowledge and experience and, in turn, refine their relationships and these spheres."[33]

In telling my personal story about crossing disciplines from religious studies to the health sciences, and my own and my study participants' experiences in undertaking Community-Based Participatory Research, I hoped to show that getting to know other worlds leads to transformative changes. Learning is not a simple process of absorbing facts, but involves a transformation, perhaps from an old self to a new person, from a depressed community to a thriving one.

Consciously and deliberately following Judith's teaching and learning process provides people the ability to cross boundaries, to imagine possibilities, and to dream and make those dreams a reality. Through a dialogical and collective effort to understand the world, from whatever academic discipline and life location, we can learn to share a core value of recognizing and appreciating our differences and cultivating our individual strengths for the common good.

[33] Ibid., 80.

REFERENCES

Alejo, Alberto E. *Tao Po! Tuloy Po!* [It's a Person! Please Come In!]. Quezon City, Philippines: Ateneo de Manila University Press, 1990.

Barnes, Linda L. "New Geographies of Religion and Healing: States of the Field." *Practical Matters Journal* (March 1, 2011). Accessed November 20, 2016. https://np.me/p6QAmj-7G.

Berling, Judith A. *Understanding Other Religious Worlds: A Guide to Interreligious Education*. New York: Maryknoll, 2004.

Birks, Melanie, and Jane Mills. *Grounded Theory: A Practical Guide*. London: Sage, 2011.

Brown, Michael. "The Sciences vs. The Humanities, a Power Struggle." *Chronicle of Higher Education*, April 11, 2011.

Greene, Maxine. *Releasing the Imagination: Essays on Education, the Arts, and Social Change*. San Francisco: Jossey-Bass, 1995.

Holkup, Patricia A., Toni Tripp-Reimer, Emily Matt Salois, and Clarann Weinert. "Community-Based Participatory Research: An Approach to Intervention Research with a Native American Community." *ANS Advances in Nursing Science* 27, no. 3 (2004): 162–75.

hooks, bell. *Teaching to Transgress: Education as the Practice of Freedom*. New York: Routledge, 1994.

Lewin, Tamara. "As Interest Fades in the Humanities, Colleges Worry." *New York Times*, October 30, 2013.

Maggay, Melba P. *Pahiwatig: Kagawiang Pangkomunikasyon ng Pilipino* [Intimations: Habitual Filipino Modes of Communications]. Quezon City, Philippines: Ateneo de Manila University Press, 2002.

Rafael, Vicente. "Your Grief Is Our Gossip: Overseas Filipinos and Other Spectral Presences." *Public Culture* 9, no. 2 (1997): 267–91.

Said, Edward W. *Orientalism*. New York: Random House Inc., 1979.

Sandelowski, Margaret. "Using Qualitative Research." *Qualitative Health Research* 14, no. 10 (2004): 1366–86. Accessed January 11, 2018. http://doi.org/10.1177/1049732304426972.

CHAPTER 4

Crossing Boundaries with Narratives: Making Space with Oral History in Community Service-Learning

Emily S. Wu

Abstract This chapter explains how oral history can be used as a strategy to empower people's voices through community-engaged service-learning. Actively listening to and documenting the oral histories of community members not only involves students in knowledge production, but also enables them to build positive cross-cultural relationships in the process. Judith Berling's signature "Open Space for Mutual Learning" approach, as well as her "Threads of Learning" process, are effective pedagogical framing for using narratives as the focus for community-based education. Applying Berling's concepts not only enhances the service-learning experiences for the students and community members, but also creates a space and process for oral history collection to serve as a form of healing.

Keywords Service-Learning · Narratives · Oral History Collection Vietnamese American · Intergenerational Communication

E. S. Wu (✉)
Dominican University of California, San Rafael, CA, USA

J. E. S. Park and E. S. Wu (eds.), *Interreligous Pedagogy*, Asian Christianity in the Diaspora, https://doi.org/10.1007/978-3-319-91506-7_4

41

Recently, I had an online chat session with Chammo,[1] who lives in a Tibetan settlement in India. In 2015, a small group of students and I lived at Menri Monastery of the Tibetan Bön tradition for a month for our service-learning course *Religion and Globalization*. Since we had a group of mostly women students, Chammo, a vibrant, bubbly young student studying in the traditional Tibetan medical school next door to our guest house, became our friend. Over the course of the month, Chammo was our guide and interpreter in the women's corners of the settlement, where the monks were reluctant, and often forbidden, to visit. She arranged for my women students to teach the forty young nuns, aged five to sixteen, in the Ani Gompa Nunnery connected to the monastery to make bracelets and dolls from colored yarn. She also recruited some of the older nuns, who were the first ones in the world to train as *Bonpo Geshemas*—the highest degree of study in the Bön tradition—for us to interview.

"Dear Sister," her typed words appeared in my chat box on the computer monitor, "I am remembering our visit to the *Ani Gompa* [Nunnery] together, and we talked to the *Anis* [nuns]. It was very important for me to listen to the *Anis* speak and translate so that you can also listen."

"The *Anis* only spoke Tibetan! We could not have understood them if we hadn't had you with us!" I reminded her.

"Yes, Sister, but it was different. The *Anis* told things that I did not know they would say, and some of them I have known for many years. They wanted to tell about their names, their work, their dreams, and what they want to be."

Then she said, "Sister, you have to write about the *Anis* and their stories. They were told and they were very important."[2]

Although this chapter is not about the *Anis*' stories in particular, Chammo's reminder—that the stories were told and they were important—is the core of this chapter about using oral history, or collecting people's own articulations of their lives and experience as a strategy to empower community members' voices through community-engaged students. Actively listening to and documenting the oral history of community members not only involves students in knowledge production, but also enables them to build positive cross-cultural relationships in the process. Berling's signature "Open Space for Mutual Learning" approach[3] as well as her "Threads of Learning" process,[4] are effective pedagogical framing for using narratives as focus for community-based education. I will use my course experiences to illustrate how applying Berling's concepts not only enhances the service-learning experiences for the students and community members, but also creates space and process for oral history collection to serve as a form of healing.

THE IMPORTANCE OF CREATING AN OPEN AND SAFE SPACE

Approaching community-engaged learning with narratives is nothing new. However, if not done in accordance with the principles of creating an open and safe space, the attempt to capture community narratives can have unintended, potentially detrimental consequences. Narratives have been utilized by service-learning educators as opportunities for students to learn about the diversity and positioning of self and others,[5] focal

---

[3] See Judith Berling, "Getting Out of the Way: A Strategy for Empowering Collaborative Student Learning," *Journal of Theology and Religion* 1, no. 1 (February 1998): 31–35.

[4] See Judith Berling, *Understanding Other Religious Worlds: A Guide for Interreligious Education* (Maryknoll, NY: Orbis Publishing, 2004).

[5] For more on helping students position themselves upon entering the community, see Margaret Himley, "Facing (Up to) 'The Stranger' in Community Service Learning," *College Composition and Communication* 55, no. 3 (2004): 416–38. Also see Nancy Welch, "'And Now That I Know Them': Composing Mutuality in a Service Learning Course," *College Composition and Communication* 54, no. 2 (2002): 243–63. For another example in establishing positionality with youths in the community, see C. T. Clark, "Unfolding Narratives of Service Learning: Reflections on Teaching, Literacy, and Positioning in Service Relationships," *Journal of Adolescent and Adult Literacy* 46, no. 4 (2003): 288–99. For insights along the same train of thought but addressing diversity more fully, see Jennifer Mitton-Kukner et al., "Narrative Inquiry in Service Learning Contexts: Possibilities for Learning About Diversity in Teacher Education," *Teaching and Teacher Education* 26, no. 5 (2010): 1162–69.

points for teaching critical reflections[6] and development of civic skills,[7] and efforts to empower students and community members.[8] Narratives are much more than personal life stories and include the larger context where the individual stories (and the storytellers) are located. Mitton-Kukner, Nelson, and Desricher articulate the utilization of narratives in a "three-dimensional narrative inquiry space" that is "composed of the personal and social (interaction), the past, present, and future (continuity) coalesced with the notion of place (situation), shaped our understandings of the field texts (data)."[9] The inquiry is conducted around the narratives, where interaction, interpretation, and contextualization are all built around the narratives, as text or data. Academic theories and analytical tools are used to "serve" or gain deeper understanding of the narratives, rather to have the narratives serve as examples to demonstrate academic theories and models.

The first formal oral history project I tried to conduct with service-learning students was a traumatic yet educational experience for the students and myself. I was very new to teaching, and also new to the complex power dynamics in the local community. We partnered with a non-profit organization that oversaw the operations of a state park that used to be a Chinese fishing village from the 1870s through the 1940s. One of the descendants of a family that founded one of the fishing businesses in the village, an elder in his late 80s (now deceased), was still

---

[6]See Nancy P. Chin, "Teaching Critical Reflection Through Narrative Storytelling," *Michigan Journal of Community Service Learning* 10, no. 3 (2004): 57–63. Also see Laura Selmo, "The Narrative Approach in Service-Learning Methodology: A Case Study," *International Journal of Research on Service-Learning and Community Engagement* 3, no. 1 (2015), http://journals.sfu.ca/iarslce/index.php/journal/article/view/98.

[7]For discussion on how using narratives in service-learning as part of pedagogy to foster student civic engagement, see Susan Robb Jones et al., "Negotiating Border Crossing: Influences of Social Identity on Service-Learning Outcomes," *Michigan Journal of Community Service Learning* 17, no. 2 (2011): 27–42. Also see Ivor Goodson, and Scherto Gill, *Narrative Pedagogy: Life History and Learning* (New York: Peter Lang, 2011).

[8]For a model of social responsibility as empowerment in service-learning, see Charles E. Jones et al., "Return to the Source: The Role of Service-Learning in Recapturing the 'Empowerment' Mission of African-American Studies," *The Black Scholar* 35, no. 2 (2015): 25–36. For a more embodied and experiential approach to empowering the community through service-learning, see Simone Ferro and Meredith W. Watts, "Dance Performance: Giving Voice to the Community," *Michigan Journal of Community Service Learning* 18, no. 2 (2012): 62–71.

[9]Mitton-Kukner et al., 1163.

living there. The elder lived in a house in the state park that was built by his family, and operated a small diner next to his house on weekends to sell simple foods and beverages to park visitors. The elder's cousin, a woman only a few years younger than he who also grew up in the fishing village, would check on him and help him run the business. I envisioned a straightforward project, mostly focused on the preservation of local culture and history. My students and I organized and digitalized the non-profit's boxes of archival materials, and found transcripts of previous interviews done with the elder and his sibling decades earlier. We visited the elder weekly to talk and learn more about him and his life. An enthusiastic member of the non-profit organization accompanied us at every visit.

After a few visits, my students and I started to feel uncomfortable, not with the elder, but with other people around him. The enthusiastic non-profit member reminded us that we were fortunate to be talking with the elder at all because other members of the organization had declared that "they had the story down." At the same time, we were told to always arrange for meetings with the elder through the non-profit, although the elder had a phone and could easily be invited in person. Furthermore, the conversations we had with the elder were always "supervised" by the non-profit member. In addition to the non-profit member's watchful guard, we also noticed that when the younger, Caucasian American friends of the elder visited, they often took on the role of answering the questions we had for the elder *for him*. The elder would sit quietly, and smile timidly, while his younger friends told his stories.

I was not prepared and therefore, unfortunately, could not prepare my students adequately for the active and collective silencing of the elder's voice that we witnessed. We also finally understood why, when we asked the elder's cousin for an interview, she sped away in her car and never looked back. She was always very kind to us, sometimes giving us cookies when we visited the diner, but also spoke very little about herself or the family's past.

The lessons my students and I learned were invaluable. We still found and heard an alternative history, one that chronicled a much more than a long-gone fishing village that was barely preserved as an outdoor museum. We heard bits and pieces of the story of a family that survived Chinese Exclusion and became mixed-race despite the anti-miscegenation law. In order to survive, the family operated several different businesses on a beach that they, as a Chinese American family, could not lawfully own but had to rent from their Caucasian neighbor. We got tiny glimpses of the history of a family that lost their grown men and were left with two generations of widows raising young children. We realized that the multiple houses built on the beach were there because, long after the Chinese Exclusion Act was repealed, people in town still would not sell houses to the half-Chinese siblings. We wished we had more opportunities, we wished we had more space, for the elder and perhaps his siblings too, to tell those stories in their own voices. An important history of Chinese experiences in racialized America was forever lost with the passing of the elder.

Jill Stauffer coined the term "Ethical Loneliness" to describe a type of abandonment by humanity where the survivors of injustice are not allowed to tell their stories on their own terms, because the rest of us fail to hear what they really experienced or how they feel about the experiences. Stauffer also articulates what I could not articulate at the time, but felt as deeply seated anger and frustration:

> A survivor whose story cannot or will not be heard is likely also someone whose harms have not yet been addressed. And if that is true, it is likely also true that social conditions do not yet exist that would make successful political transition or societal reconciliation possible.[10]

What are these social conditions that can foster genuine listening? And pedagogically, how can we create the space and, more importantly, a culture that respects such a space for safe retelling of one's own history and sincere hearing of stories as they stand? Service-learning, as a community-oriented pedagogy, means that the community is part, if not the central element, of the course experience. If the community is our classroom, or at least a key source of reference points and case studies, how can this space for genuine hearing become also an effective space for intentional learning?

Decentering the Academic vs. Community Dynamic

I first started to develop service-learning partnerships in the Asian American community in Marin County, California, with the goal of providing the undergraduate students in my general education-level

---

[10]Jill Stauffer, *Ethical Loneliness: The Injustice of Not Being Heard* (New York, NY: Columbia University Press, 2015), 32.

Philosophies and Religions of Asia course with some opportunities to observe Asian ideologies in daily practices. The goal was to situate the students within the context of a local Asian American community, where community members serve as sources of wisdom—not only on cultural knowledge and etiquette, but also on local and global histories. Later, I have offered these opportunities to students in my other service-learning courses with themes such as "Roots of Healing," "What is Humanhood?" "Structure of Power and Forgiveness," and "Understanding the Other."

Dominican University of California, where I teach and also serve as Assistant Director of Community Outreach in the Service-Learning Program, promotes a Theory-to-Practice, Practice-to-Theory model[11] where community engagement is intentionally and intricately integrated into the academic course content of service-learning designated courses. Students in these service-learning designated courses, which span a wide range of academic disciplines, are required to critically reflect on their experiences in the community. The critical reflections are not only to inform and become informed by academic contents, but also are opportunities for students to explore deeper root causes of societal issues that affect the lives of those they interact with in the local community.

Working alongside a small cohort of dedicated service-learning faculty, I have been involved in the development of the program-level learning outcomes with very clear assessment criteria. The colleagues who were instrumental in co-creating these outcomes were community-engaged faculty members who believe that we must move beyond merely having the students "being present and experiencing" the community. We set goals to ensure that our service-learning students acquire the skills to also articulate their experiences, document their observations, reflect on their own roles and responsibilities as citizens, and analyze social issues within the local context. Furthermore, in order to be more community-centered, as faculty we have challenged ourselves to decenter academic knowledge and use more community narratives as "text" for class discussion and analysis. In other words, community narratives become the core sources for contextualized knowledge and wisdom and for illuminating stories and case studies to demonstrate scholarly theories.

---

[11] See Dan W. Butin and Elizabeth Hollander, *Service-Learning in Theory and Practice: The Future of Community Engagement in Higher Education* (New York: Palgrave Macmillan, 2010).

Because I teach mostly general education and sophomore colloquia (required for all sophomore students in my school) courses with service-learning designations, my students come from all disciplinary degree programs and with varying levels of preparedness in reading, writing, and background knowledge of how to approach people from cultures not their own. Most significantly, the students come with a wide diversity of skill-based capacities, where their community engagements cannot be based on specific skill-based contributions. Also, there are many opportunities where socialization and accompaniment are the main contributions that university students can make to the community. For example, socialization may be participating and assisting in support groups and social activities, while accompaniment may be simply spending one-on-one time with one of the community members.

In this framing for community engagement, the "learning" part of the hyphenated "service-learning" is emphasized, where the "service" part occurs more on the level of cultivating the students' own sense of civic responsibility and critical awareness of relevant social issues. With the recognition that much of the learning actually takes place in the community rather than in the classroom, the content for our academic analyses also had to shift to orient more closely to the community that we work with. Participant observations and oral history collection are important, accessible tools to get closer to the grassroot level narratives on locally relevant issues.

GETTING OUT OF THE WAY AS A PRACTICE OF CULTURAL HUMILITY

Judith Berling's students from throughout her long teaching career can all attest to her exceptional ability to create open space for conversations. As a long-time observer of Berling's classroom teaching style, I have noticed a few characteristics of how her classroom management differs from conventional lecture mode. First, she creates a physical geography in the classroom where everyone, herself included, sits at the same level and around a circle (as much as the classroom and number of students allow). Second, her classes are open to students from a diversity of academic backgrounds and trainings, who in turn bring with them a wide range of expertise, perspectives, and interests. Third, Berling contributes to openness and the sense of security in her classroom by also positioning herself as an active learner and acknowledging that students often bring with them issues, concerns, and materials that she is not familiar with. Fourth, she never exempts herself from any classroom exercises; if she asks everyone a question, she also participates in contributing a response. Finally, but most crucially, she listens attentively yet patiently and allows for occasional silence as the space for additional insights to arise from around the room.

Berling calls this approach "Getting Out of the Way," where she actively aims to remove herself from the center of the learning process and allow for everyone in the room to become part of a learning community. She sees her role as "entering into the conversation as an inquirer (a fellow seeker) rather than as the font of all answers."[12] This technique is not only an effective framing to use in the classroom to decenter the faculty–student dynamic, but also a helpful framing to decenter students from the "helper-server" role in the community to more of an "engaged-learner" role. A colleague in my service-learning faculty cohort observes that "when the students realize that they don't have to be perfect and all-knowing, you can feel there is this sense of relief."[13] The sense of relief comes from the understanding that the students' responsibility, civic or otherwise, is not in proving their own worth in the community by being the bearer of knowledge and skills. The process of decentering (even if it is only for the students to understand that they are not expected to be the center of attention in the community) also allows space for students to better practice the principles of Cultural Humility[14] and Accompaniment: "To accompany someone is to go somewhere with him or her, to break bread together, to be present on a journey with a beginning and an end...There's an element of

---

[12]Berling, "Getting Out of the Way," 33.

[13]Personal communication, March 11, 2018.

[14]Cultural Humility was first introduced by nursing scholars Melanie Tervalon and Jann Murray-Garcia as an alternative to the widely institutionalized Cultural Competency approach. Criticizing the Cultural Competency approach for focusing on checking boxes of essential items as representatives of entire cultures and communities, Cultural Humility model requests that practitioners orient themselves around the principles of (1) life-long learning and critical self-reflections, (2) recognize and challenge power imbalances, and (3) advocate for institutional accountability. See Melanie Tervalon and Jann Murray-Garcia, "Cultural Humility Verses Cultural Competence: A Critical Distinction in Defining Physician Training Outcomes in Multicultural Education," *Journal of Health Care for the Poor and Underserved* 9, no. 2 (May 1998): 117–25.

mystery and openness....I'll share your fate for awhile, and by 'awhile' I don't mean 'a little while'."[15]

To concretize these principles into actual, weekly practice, I task my students with paying attention to and documenting individual stories, as well as the more collective-level narratives, in the community as a practice of active listening. Several academic skills are involved in raising many stories and a series of events to the level of a narrative: the ability to contextualize, capability to categorize and organize happenings with coherence, and the critical thinking skill to connect the events to the context. I also introduce ethnographic observations—where all human senses are used to gather information beyond verbal interactions, and minute patterns are documented for later analysis—as the tool of engagement for the service-learners. Students are required to submit weekly ethnographic field notes after each service session in the community. For their final papers, they are also required to cite from and reflect on their own field notes, which include observational details, factual data, verbatim quotes, and personal reflections from their weekly community experiences.

Oral History in the Vietnamese American Community

The Vietnamese community in Marin accounts for only 0.5% of the county's population,[16] but has one of the most established social support networks for Vietnamese ethnics in the United States. The Marin Asian Advocacy Project (MAAP), a non-profit project that supports East and South Asian communities in general, has been most actively supporting and organizing the Vietnamese community. The director of MAAP, Vinh Luu, came to Marin County in 1975 with the first wave of post-war Vietnamese refugees as a military translator and later a cultural consultant to help the refugees transition and adapt to the American setting. In the past 43 years, Luu has developed programs embedded in the county's social services infrastructure to provide culturally appropriate support for

[15] See Paul Farmer, "Partners in Help: Assisting the Poor Over the Long Term," *Foreign Affairs*, July 29, 2011, https://www.foreignaffairs.com/articles/haiti/2011-07-29/partners-help.

[16] The census count for Vietnamese ethnics in Marin is not fully accurate, because some members of the Vietnamese community are of Chinese descent and identify themselves as Chinese even though they are fluent multilinguals and participate in Vietnamese programs.

Vietnamese Americans. Most notably, as a result of long-time partnership with MAAP, in 2014 Marin County Mental Health Services created positions for Vietnamese bilingual mental health professionals to develop Vietnamese-specific support groups and criminal forensics services. With existing programs in place to insert service-learning students, there was still a need for a continuous and sustainable structure for my students that could carry through from semester to semester, as well as hopefully produce something that could benefit the Vietnamese American Community. After discussions with Vietnamese American community organizers and service providers, we started the Marin Vietnamese American Oral History Archive.

Coming from a Taiwanese immigrant family and raised in a Chinese-ethnic dominant neighborhood in the Bay Area, I am a co-learner with my students in learning about Vietnamese history, culture, and language from our local Vietnamese American community in Marin. Dominican service-learning students participate in activities and build personal rapport with Vietnamese American elders. Students attend these community programs for two hours each week. The students are guided to research and explore the sociopolitical and historical context, power dynamics, and issues that are important to these senior citizens. Toward the end of the semester, students reach out to one elder they feel most connected with and ask to conduct an interview to record the senior's own articulation of a piece of their life story—childhood memories in Vietnam, migrations to escape from wars, life as immigrants in the United States, etc.

Now in its fifth year of collection, the oral history archive is growing extremely slowly. Only a handful of students work with the Vietnamese American community each semester,[17] and to make the project truly community-centered, we do not set strict goals around "data collection." Instead, we focus on the relationships and trust built between students and elders and on creating space where the elders feel safe and empowered to tell their stories. The elders are the teachers: They own the stories of their lives, and they teach on their own terms. A few elders are open and comfortable and share elaborate accounts of their memories. A few are shy, even changing their minds in the middle of an interview to end their sessions early. Still others see that their friends have told their stories and are now itching, but also working up the courage, to tell their

---

[17]The pace of the archive project is due to limited number of Service-Learning classes and limited capacity of our community partner programs each semester.

own stories. My students and I also have only a few questions that serve as conversations starters. We respect the elders in guiding us to the part of their lives they wish to share or to the topics they want to talk about. In this open space, we have been taken on unimaginable adventures, heard heartbreaking tragedies, discovered several hidden talents, and sometimes even indulged in gossip that really should not have left the room (later edited to protect privacy). The involvement of Vietnamese interpreters has also been helpful in allowing the elders to express themselves fully; the interpreters are often crucial in enlightening us about the cultural references that may be lost if left unexplained.

The intersection between being immigrants who struggle with English and being elderly can manifest in significant internalized oppression. Recently, we had scheduled to interview one of the elders, who had been, for several weeks, excitedly anticipating for her story to be recorded. However, on the day of the interview, she repeatedly told us that her life was not interesting, her story was not worth telling, and her friends were angry with her for being so arrogant. Later, we discovered that while we were setting up for the interview, the elder's friend had joked and bullied her about being the storyteller of the day. We are still trying to find ways to create a safe and open space for the women-elders to be more comfortable—the upcoming attempt will be to ask the women-elders to let us record their demonstrations of how their favorite home dishes are cooked. Since the kitchen is traditionally the women's space, hopefully the woman-elders will find it a safer space to share their wisdom.

Threads of Learning and Empowerment

Berling's model of "Threads of Learning" describes processes that require learners (where everyone is a learner on either side of the divide), to honestly acknowledge that they do not know and recognize the impact of new knowledge of others on their own life. She also advises learners to tap into the wisdom of other learners who may be more experienced and knowledgeable in crossing that boundary. She encourages learners to develop individual relationships while being mindful of the larger structural and historical issues that differently contextualize worldviews. Finally, in a very Confucian self-cultivation fashion, she recommends that the learner internalizes the newly developed "dispositions, attitude, and character that enable one both to understand and to live in the world,"[18] only to practice these threads again. These threads, Berling proposes, are not steps with necessarily any linear progression, but that could simultaneously or separately serve to penetrate and bind approaches to decenter the learning process.

Collecting oral histories from the Vietnamese elders places them centrally as the transmitters of community history and knowledge. Within the context of these Vietnamese elders as mostly non-English speaking immigrants, much of their daily socialization focuses on acculturating them into the American society. We are merely leveling the ground to decenter the service-learning students, who are English-fluent college undergraduates, as ones who hold cultural and linguistic mastery. On the other hand, the students take on the role of ones who document and reflect, not only on the stories but also the larger context of the stories, and also become producers of knowledge.

Once I frame their community interactions as original knowledge production, the students become much more enthusiastic in their engagement with the elders. One student, who said she was never confident in her own academic capability, shared with me during class break,

> I always thought that somebody else is writing the books, and somebody else would be doing the difficult research to give us valid information. And then I'd be the one struggling to understand and trying to digest that knowledge. Nobody ever told me that I could document my experiences and that could be valid information. That's kind of mind-blowing. It makes me want to go back [to the community] every week to see what else I can find, and hear, and see, and document.[19]

The collective and continuous effort of students being present and participating in the elders' weekly social activities has also helped us gather an informal "database" of cultural knowledge to pass from one semester of students to the next. For example, one semester a good-intentioned student brought a service dog and trainer to visit the elders at the stress management group. The student thought that since therapeutic

---

[18] Berling, *Understanding Other Religious Worlds*, 80.

[19] Personal communication, November 2, 2016.

pets have been known to be well received in general, perhaps our elders would also enjoy the experience. Unfortunately, when the service dog and the trainer arrived, they immediately saw all the women quickly moving away and to the other side of the room, and they were left with the men greeting them with some awkwardness and hesitation. The room fell very silent, with none of the expected welcoming and excited petting of the dog. After some probing, the service-learning students and the second-generation Vietnamese mental health workers finally understood the reaction. In Vietnam, especially in the rural regions, dogs were not raised as pets, but as guards for homes and field. Also, the men were usually the ones feeding and raising the dogs. On the other hand, the women were always taught to be afraid of the neighborhood dogs with sharp teeth. Even the men would not consider dogs to be friendly and cuddly but rather domesticated yet potentially dangerous animals. This type of specific cultural knowledge is now passed down from one cohort of students to the next as a cautionary tale to never take contextualization for granted.

Another student shared an important teaching/learning moment in which self-reflection and cross-cultural comparison helped him understand and internalize an important cultural value in the community. He tried to offer food to the elders who had been sharing their food with him for several weeks, but they refused. Instead, they gestured for him to eat the food himself. Analyzing the situation from his own Filipino heritage as a reference point, he recalls:

Looking back, it would have been very easy for me to interpret their refusal to eat my food as a rude reaction. I have had similar experiences with my Filipino elders; they always let the younger people eat first and then the younger people usually bring them food as thanks or out of respect. I suspected a similar dynamic was at play...the more I think about it, the more I realize I share a lot of similar beliefs and traditions with these elders. I do not speak Vietnamese and only sparingly speak Tagalog. I was born in the United States; and they in Vietnam. But we both had to change in the face of American society to become something else. No matter how much I had to forget my language and the acculturative trauma I suffered, I am surprised to say I still shared a bond that transcended language and every other barrier that presented itself to me.[20]

[20] Personal communication, November 15, 2017.

Through reflecting on the interaction through the lens of his own cultural upbringing, Aaron was able to, even if only momentarily, transcend linguistic barriers and understand the elders' actions. Most importantly, he was able to genuinely feel the care behind a seeming refusal.

Over the several years of working with this community of elders, I have observed the elders teaching and nurturing the students in their own gentle ways. A student who has been working with the Vietnamese American elders for two years recounted her pleasant surprise when one elder openly thanked her for her patience and good work:

> I was completely floored by her statement, I really didn't know what to say; I was so touched. I just went over and gave her a hug. She is set to take her citizenship test soon and I almost forgot that when I first started working with this community two years ago, I tutored [this elder] with her citizenship test, basic phrases, and vocab words. I honestly was so touched I teared up a little when I got back to my car. I was always thankful to them for [sharing their stories] – it's not easy spilling your soul to a stranger, yet they do it time and time again and they thanked me for it. Crazy.[21]

Again, this is a community where intergenerational communications have been the sources of stress and conflicts. The slow yet undoubtedly growing relationship between my service-learning students and the Vietnamese elders is a sign of intergenerational reconciliation.

FINAL THOUGHTS

The Marin Vietnamese American Oral History Archive will soon be launching online to showcase interviews with the elders. Service-learning students over the last few years of our work in the community have transcribed the interviews, and the full transcripts will be available on the Web site along with the video recordings. Aside from the interpretation service provided by Marin County Health and Human Services, the project has operated with no institutional budget or funding and has relied on the accumulated relationship-building from one school semester to the next. Service-learning students have also reached

---

[21] Personal communication, February 9, 2018.

out to second-generation Vietnamese Americans in the community to gather their perspectives on intergenerational communications, particularly the transmission of cultural knowledge from one generation to the next. While there are several other Vietnamese American Oral History Archives in the United States, they feature leaders and success stories from their communities. The archive we are building in Marin will honor and feature any Vietnamese American community member who has the courage to share his/her story, regardless of social accomplishment. Even as aging members of the community, even without the linguistic capabilities to tell their stories in English, the elders should still have a safe and respectful space to tell their stories, in their own voices. We are merely being with them on their continuing journey in this foreign land that they now call home. This, however small in scale and slow in process, is also a process of healing.

REFERENCES

Berling, Judith. "Getting Out of the Way: A Strategy for Empowering Collaborative Student Learning." *Journal of Theology and Religion* 1, no. 1 (February 1998): 31–35.

———. *Understanding Other Religious Worlds: A Guide for Interreligious Education.* Maryknoll, NY: Orbis Publishing, 2004.

Butin, Dan W., and Elizabeth Hollander. *Service-Learning in Theory and Practice: The Future of Community Engagement in Higher Education.* New York: Palgrave Macmillan, 2010.

Chin, Nancy P. "Teaching Critical Reflection Through Narrative Storytelling." *Michigan Journal of Community Service Learning* 10, no. 3 (2004): 57–63.

Clark, C. T. "Unfolding Narratives of Service Learning: Reflections on Teaching, Literacy, and Positioning in Service Relationships." *Journal of Adolescent and Adult Literacy* 46, no. 4 (2003): 288–99.

Cobb, Sara B. *Speaking of Violence: The Politics and Poetics of Narrative Dynamics in Conflict Resolution.* New York: Oxford University Press, 2013.

Farmer, Paul. "Partners in Help: Assisting the Poor Over the Long Term." *Foreign Affairs*, July 29, 2011. https://www.foreignaffairs.com/articles/haiti/2011-07-29/partners-help.

Ferro, Simone, and Meredith W. Watts. "Dance Performance: Giving Voice to the Community." *Michigan Journal of Community Service Learning* 18, no. 2 (2012): 62–71.

Goodson, Ivor, and Scherto Gill. *Narrative Pedagogy: Life History and Learning.* New York: Peter Lang, 2011.

Himley, Margaret. "Facing (Up to) "The Stranger" in Community Service Learning." *College Composition and Communication* 55, no. 3 (2004): 416–38.

Jones, Charles E., Patricia Dixon, and Akinyele O. Umoja. "Return to the Source: The Role of Service-Learning in Recapturing the 'Empowerment' Mission of African-American Studies." *The Black Scholar* 35, no. 2 (2015): 25–36.

Jones, Susan Robb, Claire Kathleen Robbins, and Lucy A. LePeau. "Negotiating Border Crossing: Influences of Social Identity on Service-Learning Outcomes." *Michigan Journal of Community Service Learning* 17, no. 2 (2011): 27–42.

McNally, Michael David. "Indigenous Pedagogy in the Classroom: A Service Learning Model for Discussion." *American Indian Quarterly* 28, nos. 3 & 4 (2005): 604–17.

Mills, Steven D. "The Four Furies: Primary Tensions between Service-Learners and Host Agencies." *Michigan Journal of Community Service Learning* 19, no. 1 (2012): 33–43.

Mitton-Kukner, Jennifer, Carla Nelson, and Claire Desricher. "Narrative Inquiry in Service Learning Contexts: Possibilities for Learning About Diversity in Teacher Education." *Teaching and Teacher Education* 26, no. 5 (2010), 1162–69.

Selmo, Laura. "The Narrative Approach in Service-Learning Methodology: A Case Study." *International Journal of Research on Service-Learning and Community Engagement* 3, no. 1 (2015). http://journals.sfu.ca/iarslce/index.php/journal/article/view/98.

Stauffer, Jill. *Ethical Loneliness: The Injustice of Not Being Heard.* New York, NY: Columbia University Press, 2015.

Tervalon, Melanie, and Jann Murray-Garcia, "Cultural Humility Verses Cultural Competence: A Critical Distinction in Defining Physician Training Outcomes in Multicultural Education." *Journal of Health Care for the Poor and Underserved* 9, no. 2 (May 1998): 117–25.

Welch, Nancy. "'And Now That I Know Them': Composing Mutuality in a Service Learning Course." *College Composition and Communication* 54, no. 2 (2002): 243–63.

CHAPTER 5

Interreligious Education
for the Millennial Generation

Courtney Bruntz

Abstract The author, in this chapter, offers practical strategies (in both a large university and small liberal arts college setting) for educating students on how to become active learners in the classroom so that their conceptualization of religious worlds expands beyond stereotypes. Throughout, it explores methods the author has found successful for creating environments of active learning inside and outside the classroom space. The author discusses how to adapt Judith Berling's method for interreligious education to the millennial generation, so that students enter other religious worlds through art, texts, and narratives and continue their individualized learning by leading reflections upon such encounters. Furthermore, the chapter presents useful methods for carefully constructing contextual education that supports the student's encounter with religious traditions. The study concludes that engaged educational environments for interreligious learning complement the learning styles of the creativity seeking and collaborative millennial generation.

C. Bruntz (✉)
Doane University, Crete, NE, USA

© The Author(s) 2018   59
J. E. S. Park and E. S. Wu (eds.), *Interreligous Pedagogy*, Asian Christianity
in the Diaspora, https://doi.org/10.1007/978-3-319-91506-7_5

Keywords Active learning · Interreligious · Contextual education
Experiential learning · Flipped classroom

At the conclusion of the 2014 semester, students in my *Religion and Philosophy of Asia* class at Nebraska Wesleyan University were tasked with the challenge of acquiring perceptions of Asian religions across campus. After a semester examining diverse religious practices and philosophical viewpoints, students were challenged in this assignment to examine stereotypes of Asian traditions, to investigate the social networks that influence our imaginings of religious worlds, and to self-reflect on how their own perceptions had changed. A sampling of the questions and responses regarding Buddhism specifically revealed that Wesleyan students associate Buddhism with notions of peace, the symbol of the Dao, meditation, Kung Fu, the Dalai Lama, Jackie Chan, and of course, the "fat, happy, gold guy at Chinese restaurants." These Buddhist stereotypes are consistent with student responses from University of Nebraska-Lincoln, Oregon State University, and Doane University.

Knowing these are prevalent, over the course of a semester, I strive to construct educational spaces where my students move beyond passively consuming such stereotypes and instead actively engage, contextualize, and criticize what is disseminated to be "Asian" and/or "Buddhist." My methodology is influenced by Judith Berling's approach to interreligious education, and in the following, I take topics from Berling's work and offer the ways that I have tailored her pedagogical models to my own teaching. First, I explore ways for students to dialogue with other religious worlds; second, I analyze methods for drawing in millennial students specifically; and finally, I discuss student-centered collaborative learning. At the conclusion of this paper, I suggest that engaged educational environments for interreligious learning complement learning styles of the current seeking creativity and collaborative millennial generation.

DIALOGUING WITH OTHER RELIGIOUS WORLDS

Prior to contemporary buzz phrases in education such as "flipped classrooms" and "active learning," Judith Berling was pioneering interreligious education and focusing on student engagement. Berling's work draws on scholars from diverse disciplinary backgrounds to construct a learning theory in which students encounter other religious worlds through a dialogical process. To cross over into another religious world, students must move beyond feelings of sympathy or empathy and instead begin seeing themselves as the *other*. In "... still looking through my own cultural and experiential lenses," Berling writes, "it is important to attend to the particular words, images, and behaviors through which the other represents himself."[1] Essentially, learners must ask the questions: How do persons express, live out, understand, and articulate meaning, and what are the behaviors associated with these imaginings? This cannot be accomplished through mere descriptions; instead, students must engage the religious world in order to begin understanding sources and expressions of meaning. This is when true interreligious learning begins.

"Religious worlds" deploys a Geertzian concept of religions as cultural systems. This denotes a "historically transmitted pattern of meanings embodied in symbols, a system of inherited conceptions expressed in symbolic forms by means of which [people] communicate, perpetuate, and develop their knowledge about and attitudes toward life."[2] In an interreligious classroom, students benefit from discussions of how symbols create a synthesis of ethos across individuals, families, and collective societies. To prepare my students to interact and engage with another religious world, I set aside class time to first discuss where we each find meaning, how myths and tales, repetitious actions, family and friend relationships, etc., establish pervasive motivations for our communities and ourselves. To step into another religious world, I next introduce students to how the tradition presents itself. In a course on Buddhist Traditions, for example, it is necessary to walk students through un-learning popular conceptions of ideas such as karma and re-learning how persons within traditions involving karma express and interpret its meaning. This involves analyzing how karma translates into words, symbols, expressions, moods, and actions. Such an exploration draws students into the religious world as they acquire translation skills of key terms and symbolic expressions and begin to understand teachings as one within the tradition would.

In viewing the classroom as an extension of the outside world in my seminar courses of World Religions, I create dialogical models

[1] Judith Berling, *Understanding Other Religious Worlds: A Guide for Interreligious Education* (New York: Orbis Books, 2004), 39.

[2] Clifford Geertz, *The Interpretation of Cultures* (New York: Basic Books, 1973), 89.

for students to engage in religious worlds around them. This benefits their understanding of other religious worlds by moving the education space beyond the realm of the imagined and into the realm of the experienced. In Lincoln, NE, where I taught for three years, I strived to connect my students with religions other than their own and to do so beyond the walls of the university. Given that many of my students come into the class associating other religions with their stereotypes, I have taken numerous student groups to the Hindu Temple in Omaha, as well as the Linh Quang Buddhist Center in Lincoln. From my experience, many temples have somewhat of a set agenda when receiving guests. The Hindu Temple, for example, has a thirty- to forty-five-minute presentation that introduces students to the temple community and provides a guided tour around the main sanctum. The Linh Quang Buddhist Center in Lincoln as well has a standard program designed to greet guests and introduce them to Vietnamese Buddhism. These prearranged programs are excellent for instructors and provide students with outside the classroom learning. I have found, however, that students who do not prepare for the experience itself do not benefit as much from such contextual education as others who do. When I first began taking students to the Linh Quang Buddhist Center, for example, I provided them with information on what to expect, how to dress, proper customs, etc., but I didn't give them the tools to become active learners. I did not assign them a task for what to specifically look for while in the Buddha Hall or suggestions regarding questions to ask the community members. In terms of Berling's model of interreligious learning, while my students were physically entering a new religious world, they were not embarking on a journey of developing their own voice and agency. They were learning to respect the voices and agencies of those they were observing, but they themselves were not learning to construct individual interpretations and examinations. Without guidance, my students were unexpectedly shy, and while I knew they benefitted from "taking it all in," as they told me, I thought that there must be a better way to construct outside the classroom learning. There must be a more effective way to engage in interreligious learning while at the same time to encounter my millennial students. In this context, we must *facilitate* learning in a way that encourages students to develop their own voice by providing them with the tools to enter into meaningful relationships with practitioners of the religious worlds they are studying.

With Berling's pedagogy of dialogue in mind, I constructed a new model of contextual learning for large classes in the university setting, and I did so by creating a flipped classroom. A flipped classroom is a type of blended student-centered pedagogical model where instructors make most of the face-to-face time with students by engaging in active learning tasks to help them process and apply instructional material. Flipped classrooms have proven to be highly effective for millennial students, for they are innovative and interactive. In a traditional classroom, students are first exposed to new material in class via lecture, and then the homework following that fosters deeper understanding. In a flipped classroom, students are first exposed to new material prior to coming to class—through videos or readings. Time in class is then spent developing deeper learning of that material, and the following homework extends that learning while adding on new material for the next class. The flipped classroom guideline at University of Minnesota reads, "Flipped classrooms are a form of blended learning, a term that refers to any form of education that combines face-to-face instruction with computer-mediated activities."[3] This reinforces new material and allows students time in class to ask questions. Research conducted at San Jose State, the University of Wisconsin, and Stanford found that the most successful flipped classrooms: (1) are highly structured to the extent that time is broken down by activities and their duration; (2) include a significant amount of problem-solving, quizzing, and/or other active learning so that students are asked to apply material they encountered prior to coming to class to a particular point of inquiry; and (3) include incentives for students to complete homework and attend class.[4] Inside and outside the classroom, students are active learners. They engage with new material themselves outside the class and then develop greater understanding of that material inside the class. Thus, instructors teach new material via online lectures and within the space of the classroom, but they also *facilitate* learning via structured assignments, in-class prepared activities, and repetitious quizzing. Not only does this method of learning fit the highly active millennial population, it also provides the instructor with a means for deeply engaging his/her students. Studies have also shown

---

[3] University of Minnesota, "Flipped Classroom Field Guide," accessed April 11, 2015, http://www.cvm.umn.edu/facstaff/prod/groups/cvm/@pub/@cvm/@facstaff/documents/content/cvm_content_454476.pdf.

[4] Ibid.

that flipped classrooms produce improved educational outcomes including teaching students to problem solve, become interactive learners, and master new material on their own.[5]

In re-conceptualizing the contextual education experience to be one that invites students as participants and not merely observers, I flipped the situation so that students made the most use of the time they had at a religious site. Step one of a flipped classroom is to produce defined learning objectives and instructional strategies to determine how students will use or apply learned material. For the assignment, I created at the University of Nebraska, I divided students into eight groups. In a class of sixty, this meant groups consisted of seven or eight students. Each group visited one assigned religious community across Lincoln to observe and ask questions in order to meet the learning objective: How does a "space" become a "sacred place"? In order to apply what they had learned throughout the semester via readings and lectures, the contextual assignment required students to locate the particularities regarding sacred places. I encouraged them to contemplate: What makes this space significant to this particular religious community? What forms of expression are evident in this space, and how are they being presented? Such questions help students to engage while visiting their assigned religious location.

The second step of a flipped classroom is to familiarize students with new material. Under the learning objective in which students were investigating what makes a space meaningful to a religious community, students were required to spend time outside the classroom researching their assigned community. Throughout the semester, students had already gained familiarity with the assigned religious traditions. However, prior to attending services arranged by me, students needed to research ways in which their assigned community expresses itself through social media, Web sites, newsfeeds, etc., as well as through events and activities. Students were asked to begin constructing a sense of how the community understands itself, which also accomplishes step three of the flipped model. In this step, activities should motivate students to prepare for the educational experience—in this case, preparing for the on-site visit.

Steps four and five of the flipped classroom involve active learning strategies as well as ongoing learning. The purpose of my assigned contextual education experience is to provide a setting where students process what they have learned throughout a semester. This includes

[5] Ibid.

developing deeper understandings of: (1) a particular religious world; (2) constructions of sacred space; (3) notions of the sacred; (4) use of myths and symbols in religious life; and (5) significance of rituals for identity formation. While on-site, my students observed a religious ceremony and/or interviewed practitioners and religious leaders. Following this, with their fellow classmates and me, they shared and exchanged their experiences and also asked questions of one another: What did they notice about the ceremony? What images stuck out to them? Did they have questions that someone else in their group could answer? This learning continued after the site visit, as students worked together in groups to prepare presentations. While their final papers were to be individual ones describing place and space, presentations during finals week were collaborative.

Contextual educational experiences such as are not groundbreaking in a course on World Religions. However, what is innovative about my approach is the attention I give to the dialogical model from Berling's methodology. My students do not merely observe a religious ceremony or practice as an audience member but instead, by going through the steps detailed above, become experts on a local religious community and can enter into another religious world. The contrasts with prior experiences (where I did not use a dialogical model) were significant. Interaction with the Linh Quang Buddhist Center, for example, transformed students from passive learners to active ones, enabling them to stand with practitioners of another religious tradition. Students described being equipped to ask questions, which resulted in interesting conversations with adult members regarding the temple's history, its construction, the significance of architecture style, and the symbolic meanings of objects around the Buddha Hall. Additionally, in reflecting on the lunch they shared with temple members following the Sunday Dharma service, students discussed the warm welcome they received, and the thoughtful correlations they encountered between Buddhism and Christianity. Around the dining hall are lists of what look to be rules. Taking initiative to understand the space around them, students asked about this, wondering about the rules' meaning and why they were posted. The answer they received was: "Christianity has Ten Commandments, Buddhism has Five Precepts. They're there to remind us to follow them." This comparative invited conversation regarding similarities and differences between the two religious students, and in the presentation on the Linh Quang site, students noted their interest in how members expressed themselves, their worldview, and what it means to be Buddhist. By going through the flipped classroom process—a process that is a method for creating dialogue—students used the time at the temple to their benefit and *engaged* the religious world rather than merely observing it.

Drawing in the Millennial in the Religious Studies Classroom

Current pedagogical research is flooded with discussions regarding the millennial generation as active learners. Millennials respond well to lively class discussion, engagement with class material, and great creativity. At the same time, many of my students come to me used to being taught to a test, finding answers via a Google-search seconds away, and expecting that there is a "right" way to get an A. This challenges instructors because traditions are not monolithic and cannot be understood through a quick internet search. In survey courses, it is especially difficult to present the complexity and diversity of religious traditions without losing student interest. Further, as is noted by Berling in her discussion of interreligious learning, students encountering new religious worlds are already tempted to uphold similarities across religious traditions and/or shy away from traditions that appear too "foreign." Both situations prevent students from moving beyond the familiar and initiating encounters and understandings of another religion. I would add to this that from my experience, students are also likely to fall back on initial assumptions regarding other religions when they are not properly engaged. As a result, we must help our students understand other religious worlds beginning by tailoring teaching styles to diverse student-audiences.

Millennial students have grown up in hyper-connected multimedia environments, resulting in a low tolerance for boredom, and the generation historically represents the USA's most diverse set of students.[6] What was the result of the study? Why do you mention it here? Furthermore, millennial students feel entitled to their opinion, and value having an outlet for their voice.[7] With this being the case, discussions in various

---

[6]Neil Howe and William Strauss, *Millennials Go to College: Strategies for a New Generation on Campus* (Washington, DC: American Association of Collegiate Registrars, 2003), 7.

[7]Jean M. Twenge, *Generation Me: Why Today's Young Americans Are More Confident, Assertive, Entitled—And More Miserable Than Ever Before* (New York: Free Press, 2006), 85.

formats are effective for drawing students into engagement with class material. Five professors from Hope College in 2010 conducted six focus groups to identify models for effective classroom discussion and found that class discussions are beneficial for gaining student attention and facilitating a deeper understanding of the material.[8] However, they should be carefully constructed. Students noted that their participation in a class discussion was shaped by the professor's attitude, his/her ability to moderate discussion, the classroom atmosphere, and student behaviors and attitudes.[9] Learning styles of millennial students can be effectively adapted to interreligious learning, and this is successful through multiple forms of engagement. As noted above, discussion-based learning works well with the millennial generation. However, as also recognized above, the success of discussions, students claim, is shaped by the professor's ability to moderate. I add to this that the professor's skill in guiding discussion is vital to one of interreligious education. Entering another religious world entails:

1. Building on the diversity of learners' experience while respecting the internal diversity and multiple perspectives of religions studied.
2. Empowering learners by developing voice and agency while also teaching them to respect the voices and agencies of those whom they engage in study.
3. Entering other worlds through art, text, or narrative so that learners engage difference and particularity while acknowledging their own and others' social locations.
4. Engaging understanding and interpretation of the distinctive ways in which religions represent themselves, and not merely the mastery of ungrounded information.
5. Developing linguistic flexibility through a mutually critical conversation that engages the languages of all participants, including those of the religions studied.
6. Establishing mutually respectful relationships, learning to stand with others.[10]

[8] Patricia Vincent Roehling, Thomas Lee Vander Kooi, Stephanie Dykema, et al., "Engaging the Millennial Generation in Class Discussion," *College Teaching* 59, no. 1 (December 2010): 2–6

[9] Ibid., 3.

[10] Berling, *Understanding*, 47–48.

In interreligious learning, the professor serves as a mirror and a bridge. When confronted with a new religious tradition, students may fall back on assumptions or only perceive difference. The instructor serves as a mirror to recognize where students are located, and she/he acts as a bridge to help the student move from initial locations to new religious ones. Communication between instructor and student works well when students complete writing reflection papers, for these provide students a space to acknowledge their own social location. Professor responses back to the student provide individual encouragement for how to develop voice and agency as well as feedback on misinterpretations or translations of another religious tradition. This begins to transform the instructor into a bridge, which is developed further during class discussions. Connections as well as points of difference between religious traditions are not always obvious to the student; thus, professors during in-class discussions must initiate points of correlations. To enter a new religious world, students must be empowered to traverse the grounds linking one world to the next. My strategies for acting as a bridge for my students include encouraging them to take risks with their learning process, creating kinesthetic learning experiences to discuss Asian philosophy, and constructing (using Berling's terminology) "wild card" sessions.

Taking Risks

In her analysis of student-centered learning, Berling suggests that it is useful to create learning environments where students take risks in the learning process. I have approached this in a variety of ways. In my course on Asian religions at Nebraska Wesleyan University, students viewed the non-Buddhist film "Stranger than Fiction," and following wrote a film analysis, interpreting it based on the key teachings of Mahayana Buddhism. After weeks of reading sections of Donald Lopez's *Buddhist Scriptures*, engaging in discussions similar to the one described above, students were prepared to express the particularities of Buddhism, develop their individual voice, and learn to stand with others. Applying central Buddhist themes to a non-Buddhist film helped Buddhist traditions come alive in unique ways. Connections between images on the screen and teachings in the text were not obvious. This assignment required students to be creative, to be accurate in their understanding of Buddhist teachings, and to be precise in their interpretation. Students rose to the challenge.

I suspect, and confirmed this by asking students, that this method of engaging Asian religions worked well because it required students to do so in both an imaginative and personal way, meaning each student's interpretation of the film was uniquely their own. While an accurate level of understanding Buddhist teachings was required, how the student went about applying Buddhism to the film was specific to them, thus allowing them to personalize the assignment. Furthermore, all students, regardless of prior background, engaged Buddhist teachings in a new way.

While teaching at Oregon State University, I encouraged risk taking from my students by allowing weekly reading responses in my Asian Thought course to be completed in creative and artistic ways. Students had the option of completing a traditional paper, but should they choose to, they were able to express the teachings studied through an artistic medium, accompanied by an analysis. This openness to different modes of learning resulted in paintings, photographs, short stories, and films expressing the student's interpretation of the philosophies learned. By choosing a non-traditional medium to express their understanding, a student takes a risk. However, by encouraging them to do so, students analyzed Asian philosophy in manners exceeding my expectations. And further, they felt empowered to convey their learning in new ways.

Kinesthetic Learning

In addition to crafting assignments that students can tailor to their learning styles, I incorporate multiple learning methods within the classroom. In addition to oral and visual learning, I approach Asian philosophy through kinesthetic methods. For example, in my courses at Doane University, while presenting the differences between the individual and static True Self (Atman) in Hindu thought compared to the lesser false self—the changing ego-self—I demonstrate this comparison using a piece of candy (representing the Atman) embedded in play dough (represents the changing ego-self). While the ego-self (like play dough) is constantly changing from life to life, the true self embedded (the piece of candy) remains intact. Knowing that abstract philosophical ideas are difficult to grasp, such kinesthetic learning helps students to visualize philosophical teachings.

Wild Card Sessions

Finally, to create casual settings in which students feel empowered to ask all questions and discuss any topic, I offer "coffee shop hours" to incorporate, what Berling terms, "wild card" sessions. During these sessions, there is not a particular agenda, and students lead the discussion. I have found that more students attend such small group discussions in higher numbers than those who stop by designated office hours, for they feel they benefit from the informal conversation. Coffee shop hours occur on campus, but the discussions are in a non-academic building, exploring student-driven interests. Such exchanges outside the classroom only serve to enhance discussions within the classroom.

STUDENT-CENTERED COLLABORATIVE LEARNING

While all of the above has already introduced ways in which I strive to create student-centered learning atmospheres, I will focus on the topic specifically in this final section. In multiple articles, Berling writes about her experiences in de-centering herself and empowering students to be co-teachers and co-learners. To accomplish this is to first shift a course's objectives from what a professor will teach to what the students will learn. And within the course of a semester, the instructor's concern should not be merely providing students with expertise on the course topic, but instead helping students cross bridges to explore new concepts. In this manner, courses on religion and philosophy should thus not be merely about religious literacy but more importantly about religious/philosophical interpretation. To "get out of the way" of student-centered learning, the instructor must give up all control of the learning experience by simply providing mechanisms for students to take ownership over what is learned.

One of the most successful[11] ways I have led this form of learning is by advising student-led discussion sessions. In both large university and small liberal arts settings, in upper-level courses on Asian Thought, I dedicate class sessions to student-led small group discussions. This requires a different student each week to lead his/her peers

---

[11] Successful here refers to levels of enthusiasm students present while engaging with a new religious tradition, as well as post-semester course evaluations indicating a growth in their subject interest.

through deeper understandings of the philosophies and religious viewpoints examined, but she/he is not left unattended. I meet with the student leading the discussion prior to class time to offer suggestions. What I have found is that the most successful discussions are those that both engage students on an individual level and provide a central text or other expression of meaning, along with questions, for students to respond to. In discussing Buddhist tales, for example, a student of mine initiated conversation by having students discuss how myths (described as traditional tales) influence their own construction of identity, and which myths shape their understandings of the world. Following this, the shared text was a *Jataka* Tale (a story of the Buddha's former life). After reading the text individually, students examined basic teachings embedded in the tale, connections that this particular story has with "Chicken Little" (aka "Henny Penny"), and what teachings from the Buddha's Eightfold Path the myth reflects. This discussion model drew students into conversation very quickly, for the leader respected each student as a participant. Comparing the Buddhist tale to a known Western, one provided a bridge between cultures and helped students develop the ability to see points of comparison across religious worlds. Finally, in the examination of how the narrative reflects Buddhist teachings, students move beyond comparison and into a realm of engaging the "other."

In an Asian Thought course at Oregon State University, my class of 49 students divided into seven groups each week, with a rotating student leading discussion. In this small group setting, students came to class having completed definitions of shared terms and then discussed the reading questions together before engaging a contemporary topic related to the week's theme. Following class discussion, students submitted a reading response to me by the following Sunday evening. Berling's model of student-centered learning focuses on how to foster a joy of learning from students by creating an atmosphere in which all persons in the class (including the instructor) are "in the trenches" together. I've found that by having students lead discussions, I learn as much from them as they do from me. For example, during a week in which we examined the "deluded mind" from the Buddhist text the *Dhammapada*, a student of mine led her group through a comparison of Buddhist philosophy and Plato's *Allegory of the Cave*. While it's a comparison I encountered in graduate school, the insight and approach this young woman provided (one that included a painting she created) constructed a space for me to re-encounter the contrast, along with my students. This natural bridging between Western and Asian thought helped her classmates understand the Buddha's teachings in a manner more familiar to them and drew us all in as co-learners.

CONCLUDING THOUGHTS

Learning about other religions and philosophies is like learning new languages. But while religious worlds have common dimensions—as noted in Ninian Smart's seven dimensions—direct one-to-one translation does not capture how members of a religious world create meaning, how they understand themselves and the world around them, nor how the words, symbols, and acts serve as mechanisms for expressing oneself. Comparing religions via Smart's seven dimensions teaches students to understand religions in accordance with doctrines/philosophies, materials, rituals, individual experiences, narratives, ethics/laws, and institutions/society. This provides a useful method for religious literacy, just as sentence structure involving subjects, verbs, and objects provides a means for language learning. This method for translating religions does not, however, turn passive learners into active ones. It does not teach students to relate to another religious tradition by simply listening to the expressions of practitioners. Nor does it challenge a student to develop voice and agency in the examination of religion. Just as is required in the case of language learning, interpreting religious worlds necessitates both a guide and multiple settings. With the above, I have attempted a description of methods which have proven successful.

Because interreligious education involves moving beyond religious worlds, students who engage in this kind of study learn more about themselves and their own worldview. When one learns about another religion, the individual also has the opportunity to reflect on what she/he holds to be true. But this must be facilitated in manners that meet the student where she/he is located. Learning styles of the millennial generation fit the goals of the interreligious instructor well, for both respect the particularities of individual learners and individual religious communities. In my experience, professors of religion and/or philosophy have great opportunities to incorporate student-centered education into their curriculum and foster the goal of students as life-long learners and conscientious community members. To teach our students how to move beyond passive social interactionism and widely proliferated religious stereotypes, we are tasked with teaching them to be active learners. To do so, we must create spaces where students are not merely *exposed* to other religions but instead engage and interact with religious worlds themselves. Furthermore, we must strive to create classroom settings where this interactionism is both embraced and interpreted. Such learning situations occur within the classroom in creative ways and can be reinforced by contextual experiences. In this, we ourselves take on new roles, becoming facilitators as well as instructors.

In comparing my teaching experiences in Nebraska and Oregon, it is necessary to note that what works well in a small liberal arts setting may not work well if completely replicated in a large university institution (and vice versa). I would argue that students of liberal arts institutions are especially enthusiastic about small group and student-led discussions. The choice to attend a liberal arts school, itself, indicates that many students are prepared to have such interactions, whereas university students may choose a large institutional setting in order to experience anonymity. However, if well structured, I think students attending large universities benefit from learning from/with their peers, and by participating in small group assignments and discussions, are able to become active learners.

In the courses I teach, I begin and end each semester asking students what they imagine when they think of the traditions we study. While the beginning of a section on Asian religions will often include stereotypes of Buddhism including peace, meditation, Kung Fu, the Dalai Lama, and the "fat, happy, gold guy at Chinese restaurants," images at the end of the semester are quite different. In response to the question "Now, what do you think of when you think of Buddhism?" a student of mine responded: "Rather than thinking of 'fat, golden Buddhas,' I now imagine actions to a far greater extent than images. Rituals for instance... Bowing is a big one that I think of." While in a class on religion and philosophy we are not able to address all of the world's questions, we are able to, together with our students, construct learning environments where we reflect deeply on diverse religious worlds and come to know the "other" in a better way. I am grateful to have Judith Berling's models as a guide to implement such pedagogical strategies into my own teaching.

One suggestion: I think if you connect the concept of flipped classroom more directly to Berling's model of pedagogy and how the FC reflects or embodies her ideas in your discussion of the flipped classroom, coming back to Berling in your conclusion wouldn't seem so abrupt.

BIBLIOGRAPHY

Berling, Judith A. *Understanding Other Religious Worlds: A Guide for Interreligious Education.* New York: Orbis Books, 2004.

Geertz, Clifford. *The Interpretation of Cultures.* New York: Basic Books, 1973.

Howe, Neil, and William Strauss. *Millennials Go to College: Strategies for a New Generation on Campus.* Washington, DC: American Association of Collegiate Registrars, 2003.

Roehling, Patricia Vincent et al. "Engaging the Millennial Generation in Class Discussion." *College Teaching* 59, no. 1 (December 2010): 1–6.

Twenge, Jean M. *Generation Me: Why Today's Young Americans Are More Confident Assertive, Entitled—And More Miserable Than Ever Before.* New York: Free Press, 2006.

University of Minnesota. "Flipped Classroom Field Guide." Accessed April 11, 2015. http://www.cvm.umn.edu/facstaff/prod/groups/cvm/@pub/@cvm/@facstaff/documents/content/cvm_content_454476.pdf.

CHAPTER 6

Imprints of Hope from the Global Co-learning Classroom

Joanne Doi

Abstract Using two graduate theological courses with a specific focus on the Asian American experience as examples, this chapter explores Berling's empowerment model of teaching and learning. The first involves collaborative teaching in an interdisciplinary course of Scripture, collective memory, and the development of critical faith in the two major Asian American immigrant waves and highlights Berling's engaged pedagogy. The second course explores the co-learning environment on the Manzanar Pilgrimage, which engages the Japanese American experience of historical injury and restoration through collective memory and compassionate solidarity. Relationality is key as a community of learners is fostered during the journey through the topography of memory. Berling's methods, focusing on empowering distinctive modes of knowing and the release of a symphony of voices, fostering intercultural understanding, are highlighted in these two examples.

Keywords Engaged pedagogy · Collaborative learning · Postcolonial theory · Pilgrimage · Empowerment

J. Doi (✉)
Catholic Theological Union, Chicago, IL, USA

75

J. E. S. Park and E. S. Wu (eds.), *Interreligous Pedagogy*, Asian Christianity in the Diaspora, https://doi.org/10.1007/978-3-319-91506-7_6

One of the first courses I took as a doctoral student was Judith Berling's seminar on course design and syllabus development. At that time (1997), her teaching strategy was consciously changing from the "banking" method to a liberating or, the term she prefers, empowerment model of learning and teaching.[1] She has authored a number of reflective articles on this process, which will be referenced throughout this essay. She writes:

> I am challenged to help each student to identify and claim a distinctive mode of understanding and contribution as a legitimate option along a broad spectrum of modes of knowing.[2]

At the very beginning of the course, she introduced the class to Howard Gardner's theory of multiple intelligences which "stretched traditional understandings of human intelligence."[3] This approach aims to empower students with the gifts of intercultural learning by affirming different modes of knowing.[4] I have never been the same since, personally or professionally, as latent creative energy and insight were released within my intercultural being. As she also referenced Paulo Freire's work, we shared a similar question about transformative learning in a graduate studies context, albeit from different starting points, Berling from higher education and myself from an indigenous rural area in the southern Andes of Peru. As a Maryknoll Sister, I had just returned from a decade of overseas ministry among the Aymara indigenous people and had been actively involved with the adult popular education model, inspired by Freire's work.

The source of the title of my essay[5] places me in part in South America and that was, interestingly enough, the point of departure for

---

[1] Judith A. Berling, "Student-Centered Collaborative Learning as a 'Liberating' Model of Learning and Teaching," *Journal of Women and Religion* (1999): 43–54.

[2] Judith A. Berling, "Getting Out of the Way: A Strategy for Engaging Students in Collaborative Learning," *Teaching Theology and Religion* 1, no. 1 (February 1998): 35.

[3] Judith A. Berling, *Understanding Other Religious Worlds: A Guide for Interreligious Education* (Maryknoll, NY: Orbis Books, 2004), 21–22.

[4] See Howard Gardner, *Multiple Intelligences: The Theory in Practice* (New York: Basic Books, 1993).

[5] Michael Taussig, "Culture of Terror—Space of Death: Roger Casement's Putumayo Report and the Explanation of Torture," *Society for Comparative Study of Society and History* 26, no. 3 (July 1984): 467–97. Taussig addresses the concern with the mediation of the culture of terror through narration with the moral responsibility to not only describe a situation in ethnographic terms but toward what purpose, toward "the imprint of the gaze of hope in the space of death... to reach for another history, not only of terror but of healing as well."

my theological scholarship regarding the Asian American experience. More specifically, I was with the Aymara people of the southern Andes of Peru, 12,000 feet above sea level in the high desert plains bioregion surrounding Lake Titicaca. Together with the Aymara, an indigenous people who are often caught in sociopolitical marginalization, we lived through Peru's period of terrorism during the 1980s and 1990s. Yet over the long haul of history, they have remained defiant in their hope and tenacity for life.[6]

In Peru, I experienced what Johann Baptist Metz describes as a mysticism of open eyes, an increased readiness to perceive, to see more, not less, to name the visible and invisible suffering and pay attention to it, to be moved to compassion, to "suffer with," to be moved to respond.[7] My eyes had been opened by this expansion of love in Peru, which gave me new eyes to see the experience of my own Japanese American history (our hidden American history) and a new heart now able to perceive the suffering and hope from that time. The racialized experience of being Asian American in the USA often leaves us marginal, invisible, betwixt and between, dubbed the "perpetual foreigner" as well as the "model minority." Yet rather than a relentless search for home or a people, it is realizing that my people are all peoples, recognizing how itinerancy and fragmentation have something to do with the life and ministry of Jesus and in fact, most people.[8] It means living with ambiguity, uncertainty, and just the promise itself. It is letting go into love and finding ourselves

[6] James B. Nickoloff, ed., *Gustavo Gutierrez: Essential Writings* (Maryknoll, NY: Orbis Books, 1996), 34. Gutierrez speaks of a hermeneutic of hope: "Theology emerges at the intersection between a space of experience and a horizon of hope. The present is in its deepest dimension pregnant with the future; hope forms an inherent part of our present commitment in history. Theology does not create the vital attitude of hope out of nothing – its role is more modest. It makes these explicit and interprets them as the true lifeblood of history. It means sinking roots where the pulse of history is beating at this moment and illuminating the God of life in our midst who longs in our longing for deep fulfillment of all. This is a theology which does not stop with reflecting on the world, but rather tries to be part of the process through which the world is transformed."

[7] See Johann Baptist Metz, *A Passion for God: A Mystical Political Dimension of Christianity* (Mahwah, NJ: Paulist Press, 1998).

[8] With gratitude to Rev. Deborah Lee for this reflection. See also Deborah Lee, "Faith Practices for Racial Healing and Reconciliation," in *Realizing the America of Our Hearts: Theological Voices of Asian Americans*, ed. Fumitaka Matsuoka and Eleazar S. Fernandez (St. Louis, MO: Chalice Press, 2003), 147–57.

at home. The painfulness of our ambiguity is transformed into gift and challenge.

In articulating the goal of empowerment for students as collaborative learners, Berling summarizes what she means by this:

> Thus, "empowering learning" develops a student's voice and distinctive learning styles/modes of expressions, cultivates an ability to converse and learn in collaboration with others, links learning to the student's values and passions, fosters joy and a sense of achievement, and encourages growth through engaging new and risky challenges.[9]

The mentoring of Berling has enabled me to appreciate the resonances and approaches that I have learned from Peru, Manzanar, and Berkeley, CA, as an interdisciplinary scholar/teacher/theologian, to find my voice amidst the complexity of my intercultural being as a third-generation Japanese American woman whose young adulthood was lived amidst the Aymara people. Integration of these learnings continues to influence my teaching and co-learning in theological education, preparing ministers in and for intercultural contexts. Berling writes, "Engaged pedagogy requires building a classroom community where learning can flourish."[10] Now, I will explore two courses that I have taught: "The Bible, Memory and Asian America" and "America's Internment: Theological Pilgrimage to Manzanar."

COLLABORATIVE TEACHING

"The Bible, Memory and Asian America" was co-taught with colleague Uriah Kim (Biblical Studies), in an intentionally interdisciplinary format. Inspired by Berling's pedagogy, it was a collaborative teaching and empowering co-learning experience with us as colleagues as well as with the students. Previously, I would not have considered such an endeavor since our own personal histories reflect the different waves of migration within the Asian American flows. We brought together the two "waves"

---

[9] For detailed descriptions of these aspects, see Judith A. Berling, "Student-Centered Collaborative Learning as a 'Liberating' Model of Learning and Teaching," *Journal of Women and Religion—Expanding Classroom Walls* (1999): 43–54. See also Berling, *Understanding Other Religious Worlds*, Chapter 2 "Thinking About Learning," 18–33.

[10] Berling, *Understanding Other Religious Worlds*, 22–26.

or "watersheds" which emphasize the turning point of immigration history from Asia. I, as a Sansei (third generation) Japanese American, represent the lineage from the early 1900s (pre-1965) with my grandparents' migrations from the Meiji era Japan to the USA. Kim represents the wave of post-1965 immigration and is a 1.5-generation Korean American born in Korea and raised as a child in the USA. Prior to 1965, immigration from the Asian Pacific triangle was limited by anti-Asian immigration legislation largely based on prejudices of racial ethnic inferiority and the cultural unassimilability of Asians. The Hart-Celler Act of 1965 opened the door to a 50% increase in the Asian American population during the decades following, indicating more tolerant attitudes. Instead of a melting pot-style assimilation, recent immigration research notes adaptation to and incorporation into US society that recognizes its richness in diverse cultural matrixes. The times call for the strengthening of both cultural memory and identity precisely in order to foster new skills in relating across differences toward fruitful ongoing intercultural dialogue and living.

The course was designed to explore the intersection of the Bible, collective memory, and the development of critical faith histories from within Asian America. Amidst historical pressures of homogenization, fragmentation, and collective amnesia, what are the spiritual practices, narratives, and geographic places that reconnect us to our narratives of faith and community(s)? Understanding Deuteronomistic History from the perspective of a community resisting imperialism, collective memory studies, and Asian American literature assisted us in our pilgrimage and search. Utilizing intercultural methods and interdisciplinary skills, the course welcomed all interested. As theologian Fumitaka Matsuoka articulates, we dwell in predicament and promise as Asian Americans. The predicament involves the notions of origin, nationality, residence, and home that may shift several times over the course of a lifetime. Identity is often determined not so much by "Where are you from?" as "Where are you between?"[11] Jung Ha Kim notes, "It is not an exaggeration to say that by virtue of being alive at this particular juncture in human history, each and every one of us occupies multiple and complex social locations where boundaries and identities become increasingly uncertain,

---

[11] Peter C. Phan, "Betwixt and Between: Doing Theology with Memory and Imagination," in *Journeys at the Margin*, ed. Peter C. Phan and Jung Young Lee (Collegeville, MN: The Liturgical Press, 1999), 115–17.

displaced and fused into one another."[12] The promise is expressed well in Matsuoka's notion of holy insecurity: "Our hybrid perceptions are viewed as a state of insecurity yet holy insecurity drives the concern in API communities for empathy for the disinherited, for dignity for the hopelessly uncredentialed, and for rights for the disenfranchised."[13]

I am a descendant of two empires—Japan and the USA. This is difficult to face since the Japanese American community in the USA was marginalized through the experience of forced removal to detention camps during World War II and, at the same time, experienced "absent presence" in our classrooms and history books.[14] Resonant with the Japanese aesthetic principle of *ma*, this in-betweenness has the element of implicit potential in all concepts of separation (spatial, temporal, emotional) whereby the space between becomes the journey between.[15] Such space becomes not a moment of division but a moment of union that lends character to what would otherwise remain nondescript and colorless. It addresses the power of relatedness rather than the seeming powerlessness of being nowhere (neither here nor there). My Christian identity allows me to dwell in-between; it insists that we reach out across internal and external barbed wire fences, as both victims and offenders. Pilgrimages such as to Angel Island (part of this course) and Manzanar (a course in itself) begin to enable that reaching across in compassion.

PILGRIMAGE TO ANGEL ISLAND

A pilgrimage to Angel Island in the San Francisco Bay engaged our collective memory that we are a part of but often unaware of. Although it was billed as the "Ellis Island of the West," within the Immigration Service, Angel Island was known as "The Guardian of the Western Gate" and was designed to control the flow of Chinese, who were officially not welcome with the passage of the Chinese Exclusion Act of 1882, into

---

[12] Jung Ha Kim, "'But Who Do You Say That I Am?' (Matt 16:15): A Churched Korean American Woman's Autobiographical Inquiry," in *Journeys at the Margin*, ed. Peter C. Phan and Jung Young Lee (Collegeville, MN: The Liturgical Press, 1999), 104.

[13] Fumitaka Matsuoka, *Out of Silence: Emerging Themes in Asian American Churches* (Cleveland, OH: United Church Press, 1995), 63.

[14] Caroline Chung Simpson, *An Absent Presence: Japanese Americans in Postwar American Culture, 1945–1960* (Durham and London: Duke University Press, 2001), 2–4.

[15] Harry Wilmer, *Quest for Silence* (Switzerland: Daimon Verlag, 2000), 118–36.

the country. In reality, it was primarily a detention center. The greatest impact was on the Chinese although certain nationalities and social classes of Asians were also targeted. Nearly 19,000 Japanese picture brides were processed there by 1920; immigrants from Russia, Korea, the Philippines, and Japan were detained as were German citizens as "enemy aliens" during World War I. This engagement with spatiality as a pedagogical tool enables us to inhabit the topography of memory, to release the memories of pain and struggle but also those of hope and new life.

This topography of memory also provides a place and manner for the relationship with our dead, or ancestors of the recent past, for "to a people or culture that resists drawing clear boundaries between the dead and the living, the past and the present, self-reflections and biographies reveal stories of people, rather than of an autonomous self. ... Indeed, human identities are grounded in and through relationships with others."[16] This recovers a sense of the subjectivity that was lost due to historical erasure, invisibility, or constant misrepresentation—a viable means of reclaiming wholeness rather than producing an isolated privacy. This was experienced at even greater depth during the course that included the Manzanar Pilgrimage,[17] to which I now turn.

PILGRIMAGE TO MANZANAR

In 2006, I was invited to collaborate with the Institute for Leadership Development and Study of Pacific and Asian North American Religion (PANA at the Pacific School of Religion) and their Civil Liberty and Faith Project in teaching a course entitled "America's Internment: Theological Pilgrimage to Manzanar," which I subsequently taught for four years. As stated earlier, in Peru I had been exposed to popular education pedagogy with adult learners and wondered if these practices could converge in a graduate studies classroom for transformative learning. Interdisciplinary teaching, empowered and mentored by Dr. Berling, also emphasizes collaborative learning and shared inquiry. It seeks to provide a space of engagement and a way to promote relationality.

[16] Kim, 111.

[17] See manzanarcommittee.org for information about the annual Manzanar Pilgrimage, held the last weekend in April—co-hosted with the National Park Service.

It encourages the discovery of convergences amidst dissonance and new sources as points of departure.

During my time shared among the Aymara people, I experienced a deep connection with the Aymara through our mutual vulnerability, solidarity, and friendship. Instead of my "otherness," they recognized and embraced me as "another." The "mysticism of open eyes" engendered an expansion of love which gave me new ways to see the experience of my own Japanese American history and a new heart now able to perceive the suffering and hope that has lived in the generations of my parents and grandparents through immigration, detention, redress, and beyond. Popular religious practice among the Aymara relates profoundly with the earth, which has strengthened their resistance, creativity, and hope during centuries of oppression and colonization. Embedded with spiritual resonance through regular pilgrimages, prayer, and rituals, the land holds memory. It was in 2004 that I began a return to the land to reconnect with my own heritage by personal journeys on the Manzanar Pilgrimage, a return to the Japanese American concentration camp where my father and grandfather were detained, as well as the Japanese Catholic faith community known as Maryknoll in Los Angeles. Such pilgrimages revisit shadowed ground, uncovering sacred traces of suffering and hope. The cemetery obelisk at Manzanar expresses the message, "This is the place of consolation for all of humanity." It is about reconnection with each other, with our ancestors, with mystery, and the depth of life. It is not an escape like tourism, but rather a return to the center of pivotal events that have marked us and to narratives implanted in the land itself. Land holds memory. The pilgrim's journey seeks a restoration of wholeness by a re-centering, reentering, and recovery of history as well as a recovering from history[18]; it is a rediscovery that we are part of a living and vital collective memory. Companions on the journey, we experience more together than we could alone.

MOTIVATION AND PREPARATION

I expected perhaps a half-dozen Asian/Asian American seminary students to register for the course but had to close the class at twenty students who came from very diverse ethnic backgrounds. As we moved

[18] Karen L. Ishizuka, *Lost & Found: Reclaiming the Japanese American Incarceration* (Urbana and Chicago: University of Illinois Press, 2006), 173–92.

through understanding and experiencing the four phases of the pilgrim-age process, narrative connections were shared. The first phase of pilgrimage, motivation and longing, revealed a widespread wounded-ness: Local Californians had heard stories from their parents about friends and neighbors being taken away or simply disappearing from their classrooms. Those from the Midwest and East Coast felt haunted by this dissonant history that was not taught in schools, as if it never really happened. The commitment to journey together to shadowed ground was shared in the longing to reclaim lost parts of ourselves, to reconnect and to reconcile. What I had limited to being a Japanese American story was revealing itself as an American story that has meaning for wider circles of communities and generations. We reenter into the chaos of suffering and its lack of interpretability precisely in order to give voice to both the suffering and that which made the suffering bearable, resisting the challenge of emotional meaninglessness.

To provide context for the journey, during the second pilgrimage phase of preparation and departure, we studied significant facts of Japanese American history: the Executive Order 9066 that set mass detention in motion, the Civilian Exclusion Orders, and the "evacuation" of 120,000 people initially to assembly centers to await transfer after the completion of ten "relocation centers" (detention centers or concentration camps) in remote areas of the country, often on Native American land.[19] We were fortunate to have living survivors in the area who were able to share memories of their experience. We collaborated with two local historical Japanese American churches, Buena Vista Methodist Church in Alameda, CA, and Sycamore United Church of Christ in Albany, CA. Through sharing their stories accompanied by circles of respectful listening, healing and new co-learning happened for the survivors and the students. The commitment to journey to Manzanar and understand what happened continues to release that which has been shrouded in silence for many years and, paradoxically, brings new wholeness in knowing more of the entire story, which is still emerging. The survivors would bless and thank us for the journey we would be making. In many ways, the immersion and experiential aspects of the course began before the actual physical journey to Manzanar.

---

[19] Please refer to the many historical resources now available regarding the Japanese American internment period.

Preparation also involved spiritual practices that freed us to tempo-
rarily suspend status quo or social markers in order to be able to cross
a threshold and enter into liminal space and time. Simple embodied
gestures in silence were developed: listening, remembering, mourning,
honoring, and sharing/solidarity. These were invoked and practiced
together at different moments during the course: in response to the survivors' stories, during classroom sharings, at different places at Manzanar
such as the gardens, the latrines, mess hall locations, the children's vil-
lage/orphanage, and the obelisk at the cemetery during a dawn prayer.
Theological preparation provided a means to reflect on suffering, mourning, memory, and hope. The losses endured that cannot be recovered
require the ability to mourn rather than be forgotten, compromised, or
sacralized. The memory of suffering grounds hope as it counteracts nos-
talgia and historical triumphalism, which causes forgetfulness or opacity.
Metz writes "resurrection mediated by way of the memory of suffering
means: the dead, those already vanquished and forgotten, have a meaning which is yet unrealized."[20]

THE JOURNEY

The third phase is the journey itself, which, in a practical sense, meant an
eight-hour bus trip south through the Central Valley, across the Mojave
Desert and up the eastern side of the Sierras to arrive at the Manzanar
National Historical Site, located between the towns of Lone Pine and
Independence and now in the care of the National Park Service. We
made the journey with heightened sense of sight, sound, taste, touch,
and smell, our ability to perceive. We journeyed to a "thin place" where
the boundaries are more porous and permeable between the visible
world of our ordinary experience and the encompassing Spirit-Sacred-
God that is present everywhere, though we often do not perceive
it. "Thin places" is a metaphor that concerns anywhere our hearts are
opened. Dusk and dawn, mountains and high places, music, poetry, lit-
urgy, literature, the visual, and theater arts are some of the many kinds
of thin places. Certain people are thin places where we experience the
spirit's presence. Serious illness, suffering, and grief have the potential
to become thin places when our hearts are broken open by such experiences rather than closed down. Yet how do we rise with our hearts that

[20] Johann Baptist Metz, *A Passion for God*, 65.

feel simply broken from something such as the historical injury of intern-ment? How do we collectively enable, empower each other, and journey together to name the wound, mourn well, in order to live into the pro-cess of transformation?

This is what we were co-learning, discovering, and experiencing together. We joined with over 700 other pilgrims converging during the last weekend of April for the annual Manzanar Pilgrimage. The week-end involves a program of historical awareness, making the connections relevant today for similar situations (executive orders, Arab and Muslim Americans, undocumented immigrants, Syrian refugees), and an interreli-gious ceremony (Buddhist, Christian, Shinto, Muslim) to honor the dead that evoked layers of meaning, collective memory, healing, and ongoing commitment to reconciliation, justice, and compassion. It is a journey that frees the pilgrim from all that prevents heart-unity with others, where we experience *communitas*. There, in the hot desert sun by the cemetery obelisk, with Mt. Williamson standing in the background, we gathered to remember, to mourn, to listen, to pray, to dance *obon*—the dance with our dead—with hope and gratitude for the imprints of compassion on our hearts. We literally encountered imprints of hope in the stone and water-fall gardens created by the internees for the contemplation of restorative beauty amidst the unjust desert incarceration—the unfailing stream of integrity, the flowing waters toward justice. Imprints of hope: birdsong on barbed wire. Dawn and dusk at Manzanar, communion with the living and the dead. Echoes of children's voices both past and present. Youth reaching out across the barbed wire realities of today. Elders and ancestors passing on wisdom and strength for the journey.

RETURN AND PROMISE

The fourth phase is the return and promise, and it is a challenging period. We are changed by the experience and come away with new wis-dom and awareness, moved to prayer and action. What do we bring back to the community? How do we fulfill a promise of social responsibility that was inspired by the journey? A Filipino student broke through the enmity of war by connecting the suffering of her people at the hands of the Japanese military with the suffering of Japanese Americans in the USA during World War II. Many participants discovered friends and rel-atives who had been detained at Manzanar on the wall cloth of 10,000 names, and confirmed by a cell phone call, that yes, your uncle was there, but we just never talked about it. Solidarity with the Arab American community in the aftermath of 9/11 deepens as parallel connections are made, revealing the similar pattern of targeting those who "look like the enemy." In today's political climate, connections would be made with the impact of an Executive Order that is experienced again with a different target group yet similar suffering, solidarity, and resistance. Final "projects of promise" included homilies, radio interviews of church members who came forward with their stories of detention and survival, prayer services with images from the pilgrimage, solidarity projects with undocumented immigrants, research papers concerning the spirituality of social movements, the connection with the 1965 United Farm Workers' Pilgrimage from Delano to Sacramento, Native American layers at Manzanar, reflections on "church on the bus" and intercultural faith communities, lesson plans on the Manzanar experience, and for many an ongoing commitment to participate in the annual Manzanar Pilgrimage as well as search out other sacred places of our lived experience.

Conclusion

To circle back to the beginning of this essay, empowering distinctive modes of knowing and empowering release of one's authentic voice has a multiple effect in the atmosphere of co-learning. As evident in the projects of promise, a symphony of voices and insights emerges with resonant and dissonant harmonies, in major and minor keys, sharing the journey together toward transformation that is personal, collective, and global. Judith Berling writes about the discovery of her vocation:

> ...my deepening sense of the injustice and ignorance of racism was dramatically juxtaposed to the broadening of my cultural and spiritual horizons in the course on China. I had discovered a "vocation," a significant lifetime undertaking. It became clear to me that through learning and teaching about China I could seek to perform a ministry which would work at eroding the foundations of racism and building the foundations of cross-cultural understanding. ...I sought to become a cultural bridge, one who could "translate" and "interpret" Chinese cultural values and beliefs in ways that would help others see their value and appreciate their contributions to the global heritage.[21]

[21] Judith A. Berling, "Seeking Common Ground: Models for Understanding and Negotiating Religious Diversity," *The Cresset Easter* (1998): 6.

Berling's vocation, teaching, and scholarship have had a ripple effect in widening circles, indeed building the foundations of cross-cultural and intercultural understanding. It is boundary crossing to reconnect that which was fragmented. To you Judith, I express gratitude by saying "*Yoroshiku o negai shimasu*,"[22] which I liberally translate as goodwill toward the future of our meeting again, knowing that our relationship holds good things in the future, ongoing co-learning.

BIBLIOGRAPHY

Berling, Judith A. *A Pilgrim in Chinese Culture: Negotiating Religious Diversity*. Maryknoll, NY: Orbis Books, 1997.

———. *Understanding Other Religious Worlds: A Guide for Interreligious Education*. Maryknoll, NY: Orbis Books, 2004.

———. "Getting Out of the Way: A Strategy for Engaging Students in Collaborative Learning." *Teaching Theology and Religion* 1, no. 1 (February 1998): 31–35.

———. "Seeking Common Ground: Models for Understanding and Negotiating Religious Diversity." *The Cresset Easter* (1998): 5–11.

———. "Student-Centered Collaborative Learning as a 'Liberating' Model of Learning and Teaching." *Journal of Women and Religion—Expanding Classroom Walls* (1999): 43–54.

Gardner, Howard. *Multiple Intelligences: The Theory in Practice*. New York: Basic Books, 1993.

Ishizuka, Karen L. *Lost and Found: Reclaiming the Japanese American Incarceration*. Urbana and Chicago: University of Illinois Press, 2006.

Kent, Corita, and Jan Steward. *Learning by Heart: Teachings to Free the Creative Spirit*. New York: Bantam Books, 1992.

Kim, Jung Ha. "'But Who Do You Say That I Am?' (Matt 16:15): A Churched Korean American Woman's Autobiographical Inquiry." In *Journeys at the Margin*, edited by Peter C. Phan and Jung Young Lee, 103–12. Collegeville, MN: The Liturgical Press, 1999.

Lee, Deborah. "Faith Practices for Racial Healing and Reconciliation." In *Realizing the America of Our Hearts: Theological Voices of Asian Americans*, edited by Fumitaka Matsuoka and Eleazar S. Fernandz, 147–57. St. Louis, MO: Chalice Press, 2003.

---

[22] The Japanese phrase "*O negai shimasu*" translates "I am in your care. Please let me train with you. Please teach me." asking the other person to teach you, and that you are ready to accept the other person's teaching. In Aikido, it affirms the co-learning atmosphere of the practice. "*Yoroshiku o negai shimasu*" is used at the end of something written and literally translates "I'm hoping that our relationship holds good things in the future."

Matsuoka, Fumitaka. *Out of Silence: Emerging Themes in Asian American Churches*. Cleveland, OH: United Church Press, 1995.

Metz, Johann Baptist. *A Passion for God: A Mystical Political Dimension of Christianity*. Mahwah, NJ: Paulist Press, 1998.

Nickoloff, James B., ed. *Gustavo Gutierrez: Essential Writings*. Maryknoll, NY: Orbis Books, 1996.

Simpson, Caroline Chung. *An Absent Presence: Japanese Americans in Postwar American Culture, 1945–1960*. Durham and London: Duke University Press, 2001.

Taussig, Michael. "Culture of Terror—Space of Death: Roger Casement's Putumayo Report and the Explanation of Torture." *Society for Comparative Study of Society and History* 26, no. 3 (July 1984): 476–97.

Wilmer, Harry. *Quest for Silence*. Switzerland: Daimon Verlag, 2000.

CHAPTER 7

Critical Engagement: Integrating Spirituality and "Wisdom Sharing" into Higher Education Curriculum Development

Elizabeth Stanhope Gordon

Abstract This chapter proposes expanding Berling's interreligious approach to one that can embrace the learning process of encountering difference for higher education students who identify as either religious or non-religious. An expanded approach incorporates a pedagogy which explicitly recognizes the transcendent or spiritual aspects of human experience outside of a religious framework. Rather than viewing Christianity, theology, and interreligious learning as elective subjects, a critical framework of spirituality, wisdom, and wisdom sharing can become an integral part of higher education curriculum development across disciplines. As pluralism increases in our society, a greater need arises for an appreciation and understanding of our common humanity. This expanded approach allows for student growth in cross-cultural values, such as mutuality, compassion, empathy, and justice as well as for an increased awareness of religious and non-religious wisdom traditions that promote individual and communal well-being.

E. S. Gordon (✉)
Seattle University, Seattle, WA, USA

© The Author(s) 2018
J. E. S. Park and E. S. Wu (eds.), *Interreligous Pedagogy*, Asian Christianity
in the Diaspora, https://doi.org/10.1007/978-3-319-91506-7_7

Keywords Spirituality · Wisdom sharing · Curriculum development
Cross-cultural values · Transcendent level · Non-religious

This chapter proposes expanding Judith Berling's interreligious approach
to one that can embrace the learning processes of students who identify
as either religious or non-religious and who are interested in professional
fields other than theology or religious studies, such as education, business, nursing, or engineering. The alternative suggested here uses spirituality rather than religion as the organizing concept, and wisdom sharing
rather than interreligious learning to describe the educational process.
With this expanded approach, we are able to transfer the insights of
Berling's interreligious learning theory to mixed spaces of religious and
non-religious students inside and outside of a religion-specific class.

To start, we must clarify the terms *spirituality* and *wisdom sharing*.
Spirituality is often defined as what gives meaning or purpose to life.
However, a more nuanced definition will help us engage religious and
non-religious participants in identifying their own values and dialoguing
with diverse others. Critically thinking about spirituality requires a definition that incorporates multiple levels of our humanity: physical, psychological, cultural, and transcendent. In my research, spirituality embodies
the contextualized values, beliefs, and practices expressing an orienta-
tion to and a process of perceived human flourishing found in individual, communal, and transcendent connections to reality.[1] Communal
connections occur through a shared history, the shared language of a
text, with other individuals, or as part of a larger culture or tradition.
Transcendent connections correlate to a transcendent level of relations
that draw us to participate in a greater whole. This level emerges out of
and carries beyond cultural interactions. Positive values leading to unity
across difference, ethics, a higher power, and divinity all characterize

---

[1] This definition is drawn from multiple sources. See Donald Gelpi, *The Gracing of
Human Experience: Rethinking the Relationship Between Nature and Grace* (Collegeville,
MN: The Liturgical Press, 2001); Mark Graves, *Mind, Brain, and the Elusive Soul:
Human Systems of Cognition and Spirituality* (Burlington, VT: Ashgate Publishing,
2008); David Kyuman Kim, *Melancholic Freedom: Agency and the Spirit of Politics* (New
York: Oxford University Press, 2007); and Carlyle F. Stewart III, *Black Spirituality and
Black Consciousness: Soul Force, Culture and Freedom in the African-American Experience*
(Trenton, NJ: Africa World Press, 1999).

transcendent-level relations.[2] Most people do not speak in terms of identifying their "spirituality," but by looking at how people define supportive communities, passions, and hope, we can point to their perception
of human flourishing or thriving and how they live out this perception
through values, beliefs, and practices.[3]

Wisdom, which articulates the individual and communal insights
gained from reflection on and interpretation of life experiences, is fil-
tered through spirituality. These life experiences may include knowledge
from a sacred text and religious community, an oral tradition on living in
balance with others, or expertise gained in a practice, craft, or particular
social role.[4] Wisdom sharing refers to the acculturation, or experiential
and collaborative learning process, which occurs through mutual engagement with others and the exchange of personal or traditional insights
drawn from living a fulfilling life.[5]

Berling discusses wisdom explicitly, and wisdom sharing implicitly, in
her discussion of acculturation and the transforming *habitus*, or disposi-
tion of wisdom toward greater understanding, it produces.[6] In addition
to reflection and interpretation that shape wisdom, the "tools" adapted
from Berling's interreligious approach incorporated here illustrate

---

[2] Graves, 129.

[3] "Human flourishing" refers to traditions or collective practices to enhance the quality
of life.

[4] This definition of wisdom is drawn from the following sources: See Judith Berling,
Understanding Other Religious Worlds: A Guide for Interreligious Education (Maryknoll,
NY: Orbis Books, 2004), 52–53; Monika Ardelt, "Empirical Assessment of a Three-
Dimensional Wisdom Scale," *Research on Aging* 25, no. 3 (2003): 273–84; Susan
Chatwood et al., "Approaching Etuaptmumk: Introducing a Consensus-Based Mixed
Method for Health Services Research," *International Journal of Circumpolar Health*
74 (2015), https://doi.org/10.3402/ijch.v74.27438; Willem Lemmons, "Hume and
Spinoza on the Emotions and Wisdom," *Scottish Journal of Philosophy* 3, no. 1 (2005):
47–65; and Nancy Turner et al., "Traditional Ecological Knowledge and Wisdom of
Aboriginal Peoples of British Columbia," *Ecological Applications* 10, no. 5 (October 2000):
1275–87.

[5] See Berling, 29.

[6] Berling, 52, citing Edward Farley, *Theologia: The Fragmentation and Unity of
Theological Education* (Philadelphia: Fortress Press, 1983), xi. Berling states, "The formation of *habitus* includes both cognitive understanding and patterns of relationship and
behavior. This *habitus* is ... 'a sapiential and personal knowledge'." "Sapiential" refers to
wisdom. See, generally, Berling, 53–60.

wisdom sharing to include mediating language,[7] a bi-focal view,[8] and accountability.[9] These tools will be discussed in more detail later in the chapter.

The challenge in curriculum development with a framework of spirituality and wisdom sharing will be twofold: (1) recognition that religious wisdom and non-religious wisdom contain a dynamic that goes beyond culture to a transcendent level articulated through values, beliefs, and practices that unify across difference; and (2) a willingness to incorporate into an institutional pedagogy philosophical tools and concepts that affirm our humanity as part of an interrelated, interdependent whole. Our students today are not just Christian learners of other religions.[10] Whether the classroom is in a religious or secular university, students represent an array of religious and non-religious affiliations, from Christian and Buddhist to secular humanist, scientific materialist, and the catch-all, "spiritual but not religious."[11] Many identify with multiple cultural traditions.

Moreover, few of these students plan to go into the fields of theology or religious studies. Their fields of study range broadly from the humanities and social sciences to the arts, nursing, business, engineering, and science. To constructively impact the imaginations of both religious and non-religious individuals for the purposes of learning through difference

---

[7] Mediating language comes from transitional terms used "to mediate the boundaries" of difference in cross-cultural engagement. See Berling, 31, citing Kenneth A. Bruffee, *Collaborative Learning: Higher Education, Interdependence, and the Authority of Knowledge*, 2nd ed. (Baltimore: John Hopkins University Press, 1998), 47. For example, "love" or "mystery" might be mediating language for the God of Christianity in speaking with non-religious students.

[8] As discussed later in the chapter, Berling uses the terms synaptic vision and localized context rather than bi-focal view. Bi-focal view points to the clarity of perception that occurs when we consider a particular, lived context together with an interconnected, transcendent whole. Our understanding then embraces being both the "near-sighted" and the transcendently "far-sighted."

[9] Accountability indicates the extent to which learning across difference changes one's *habitus*. See Bering, 52–53.

[10] Although not expressed in Berling's book, she regularly incorporates interreligious learning in her graduate seminars which are made up of students from diverse religious traditions. If we continue to label the framework for dialogue as "interreligious" or even "interfaith," that labeling can signal to potential participants the necessity of holding a religious worldview beyond a non-religious or secular one.

[11] See Terrence Tilley, *Faith: What It Is and What It Isn't* (Maryknoll, NY: Orbis Books, 2010).

requires a more expansive category of the human condition than inter-religious, secular, or multicultural, as well as a rationale for integrating such a category across disciplinary fields for both students and faculty.

SPIRITUALITY AND WISDOM AS A COMMON THREAD

If we step away from the particularized identity associated with a religious tradition and look at the spirituality of human flourishing underlying that tradition, we find common transcendent-level values shared with the spirituality of non-religious cultural practices and traditions. These common concepts often include an interconnected view of the earth and its human and non-human inhabitants, an appreciation for love, peace, beauty, and justice and recognition of the need for humility in engaging with others. How each of these values may be applied within a particular tradition will certainly differ and may include a higher power or a specific representation of divinity.

Wisdom sharing also draws from religious and non-religious sources, frequently through written or verbal storytelling and sometimes through engaging in a practice.[12] These stories contain a broad range of information on problem-solving, culture, and experiential knowledge in how to treat human and non-human others and maintain relationships. Because wisdom sharing comes from many cultures and often occurs in the form of stories, it does not produce the same type of skepticism found among non-religious students required to take a Christian theology class. Thus, wisdom sharing provides a more inclusive means of communicating transcendent-level connections than the potentially exclusive Christian-identified term of theology.[13] Moreover, theology and wisdom derive from similar processes. Wisdom comes about through reflection on and inter-pretation of life experiences through a lens shaped by a transcendent-level value or relationship and tested against community norms.[14] Similar to interreligious learning, participants in wisdom sharing must have a

---

[12] The Christian Gospels exhibit this type of wisdom as do many sacred texts and oral traditions.

[13] In some contexts, and among many of my students, the term, "theology," is not exclusive to Christianity. See also Monica Coleman, "Speak Like Christ, Adorn Like Plaskow: Embodied Theologies," *Journal of Feminist Studies in Religion* 33, no. 2 (2017): 105–9.

[14] See Yang Guorong, "Transforming Knowledge into Wisdom: A Contemporary Chinese Philosopher's Investigation," *Philosophy East and West* 52, no. 4 (October 2002): 443; Monika Ardelt, "Wisdom and Expert Knowledge System: A Critical Review

willingness to encounter difference, interpret what is communicated, reflect on it, and own their response.[15] Finally, as a function of interdisciplinary work, the value of wisdom is recognized across multiple disciplines.[16]

If we, as educators, are to help our students know how to build bridges across "significant difference" and work together, we must provide constructive experiences for them to become aware of their identities and biases and become grounded in their own self-identified traditions of human flourishing.[17] Because the transcendent connections explicitly identified in spirituality create unity across difference but do not require a unity of shared beliefs to do so, intentionally incorporating classroom exercises that bring greater awareness to transcendent connections can support efforts to create greater understanding and address inequity, injustice, and unequal interpersonal power dynamics.[18]

From my experience, an approach based on spirituality and wisdom sharing has been productive in supporting acculturation, or collaborative learning across difference, in leadership, nursing, and business classes, as well as in theology and religious studies. As students grow in their capacity to authentically tell their own particularized stories, especially in

---

of a Contemporary Operationalization of an Ancient Concept," *Human Development* 47 (2004): 260.

[15] A more detailed description of such engagement is Critical Engagement, a method I developed for ethnographic research using a hermeneutic of experience: (1) Through mutual dialogue, identify the intersectional particularity of the person to be engaged; (2) Identify the intersectional particularity of the interpreter; (3) Locate the difference in meaning or "otherness" of the expression or situation that is being interpreted; (4) Determine the predominant significance of what is being interpreted for the engaged person and for the interpreter: historical, spiritual, biomedical, the nature of humanity, the nature of divinity, etc.; (5) Evaluate the expression or situation in light of this information with an awareness of the interpretive lens being used—if the significance of the expression is a spiritual one, etc.; and, (6) Appropriate the meaning—decide how the meaning given to an expression or a situation influences future behavior or communication for the interpreter toward the engaged person in recognition of their mutual humanity (functionality of interdependence). This method has been influenced generally by the works of Donald Gelpi, Robert Goizueta, Robert Lassalle-Klein, and Sandra Schneiders.

[16] Besides theology and religious studies, the research spans philosophy, sociology, public health, and ecology. See footnote 4, above.

[17] See Berling, 24–25, 39–40 in stressing the pedagogical importance of spiritual growth, empowerment, and including all voices.

[18] For example, in nursing, spirituality and wisdom sharing have been used to address patient–provider communication deficits which led to inadequate interpretation of patient histories and diagnostic assessments.

relation to the stories of others, their sharing reveals a larger, more comprehensive narrative of learning and the significance of it for culturally competent higher education curriculum development. Although a framework of spirituality and wisdom sharing may be more inclusive, this does not diminish the difficulty in raising awareness of transcendent-level values and connections outside of religious language. The difficulty in defining transcendent experience points to its emergent quality beyond that of culture and its integrated, relational existence in the embodied human experience. Just as individuals participate in culture, individuals and cultures participate in transcendence.[19] Our participation involves immeasurable variations. Thus, we can experience transcendent connections, but our capacity to research, define, and control the transcendent level will be limited.

Once recognized, this limitation can have a liberating effect, particularly for students from marginalized cultures, which are often defined by more powerful, dominant ones. By acknowledging that all faiths, traditions, and individuals, religious or otherwise, have transcendent relationships that can be approximated but not fully articulated, we can see that one interpretation of transcendence cannot be definitively qualified by an oppressive other. Spiritual concepts and descriptions within a cultural context cannot be colonized or dismissed by a more dominant culture in which we all encounter and engage transcendent-level relations as "minor traditions."[20] Even where dominant cultures have tried to obliterate the spiritual traditions of marginalized cultures, that effort has been unsuccessful.[21]

The wisdoms of ancient religious traditions have long recognized the futility of fully knowing or describing the transcendent divine in

---

[19] Graves, 129.

[20] See William Connolly, "Europe: A Minor Tradition," in *Powers of the Secular Modern: Talal Assad and His Interlocutors*, ed. David Scott and Charles Hirschkind (Palo Alto, CA: Stanford University Press, 2006), 75–92.

[21] Emilie M. Townes, *In a Blaze of Glory: Womanist Spirituality as Social Witness* (Nashville: Abingdon Press, 1995), 114–16. Townes describes "traditioning" in the context of African-American spirituality from times of bondage to the present as, "passing on legends that affirm strength and righteous agency in the miasma of oppression." See also, Suzanne Crawford O'Brien, ed., *Religion and Healing in Native America: Pathways to Renewal* (Westport, CT: Praeger Publishers, 2008). Both of these texts contain types of wisdom sharing.

sacred texts. In more contemporary texts, participatory research models involving indigenous knowledge introduced a consensus-based mixed method for health service research, *Etuaptmumk* or two-eyed research, with spiritual values of humanity, respect, and kinship among the stated research values.[22] *Inuit Qaujimajatuqangit*, a government recognized indigenous knowledge public health database in Nunavut, Canada, specifically includes a spiritual domain and *cannot* be reduced to a "cultural artifact."[23] Acknowledging these transcendent connections of spirituality as integrated into our humanity, as well as the difficulty in "capturing" a single, secure cross-cultural description, means that instructors will require "tools" that create space for the experiential and collaborative learning of wisdom sharing. Fortunately, the tools that Berling has developed adapt quite well.

PEDAGOGICAL TOOLS FOR CURRICULUM DEVELOPMENT

The tools used to promote understanding and collaborative learning that I will focus on mediating language, a bi-focal view, and accountability. Throughout the rest of the chapter, we will see how these tools can be used with a framework of spirituality and wisdom sharing and incorporated into curriculum development.

Mediating Language

Berling describes the components of understanding as gathering facts and information, recognizing one's own culture and perspectives, and then finding mediating or transitional language for understanding the other with whom one is in dialogue. She mentions the importance of mediating language as a tool for interreligious learning where

---

[22] Susan Chatwood et al., "Approaching Etuaptmumk: Introducing a Consensus-Based Mixed Method for Health Services Research," *International Journal of Circumpolar Health* 74 (2015), https://doi.org/10.3402/ijch.v74.27438.

[23] See S. Tagalik, *Inuit Qaujimajatuqangit: The Role of Indigenous Knowledge in Supporting Wellness in Inuit Communities in Nunavut*, National Collaborating Centre for Aboriginal Health (Prince George, BC: University of Northern British Columbia, 2009). Within the USA, publicly funded behavioral health services recognize psycho-socio-spiritual factors as critical to recovery, yet a quantitative-dominant research approach largely limits inquiry into positive feelings of self and others.

vocabulary and concepts may not translate well from the religious world of one learner to another.[24] By recognizing that human interactions include a transcendent level of connections, frequently articulated through religious traditions but also experienced by non-religious individuals, we can begin to create mediating language that allows deeper engagement among all students in classrooms and about issues vital to our world.

A spirituality framework provides general categories that can mediate concepts, speaking to both religious and non-religious individuals. Within this framework, wisdom sharing can provide more accessible specificity. Accessible specificity refers to the ability of a story to illustrate one or more of the general categories of spirituality and to do so in a way that its wisdom can be mutually appreciated without requiring a unity of shared beliefs. Wisdom sharing needs to be accessible because as students increasingly identify as non-religious in an individualized and secularized culture, they are wary of perceived attempts by family members, instructors, or cultural authorities to insist on any type of religious belief system, particularly Christianity with its historical social privilege. Conversely, without accessible specificity, students may then become isolated from resources and communities with shared language, concepts, and identities explicitly related to transcendent-level systems, such as institutionalized religions and ancient cultural traditions.

Descriptions of spirituality often fall into one or more of the following three categories: community, passion, and hope. All three categories can be used to provide a structure in considering individual or communal spirituality in terms of values, beliefs, and practices; perceived traditions of human flourishing; and, individual, communal, and transcendent connections to reality. In describing community, one identifies a sense of identity and belonging and a way of being part of a larger whole. A community provides support and accountability toward human flourishing in a particular way. Community may appear in the form of a beloved text, a dear friend, a family, a public space where one is seen regularly, or a cultural, religious, or spiritual community. Passion motivates and gives us drive to engage with what we are passionate about even when to do so may be inconvenient, difficult, or life-threatening. Passion provides a sense of

---

[24] Berling, 39–40.

purpose and focuses our creativity and inspiration. We have multiple passions, which may change over the course of time. For example, a nursing student may have a passion for healing as well as for the well-being of her family. Finally, hope embraces the trust and confidence that real future possibilities exist and can be attained, often within an identified framework of reliance on the greater whole or synoptic vision.[25]

Additional mediating language can be considered at the more detailed level of the functional and substantive impacts of spirituality on individuals. The functional impact often evidences itself physiologically, such as feeling calm or less anxious. The substantive content or beliefs associated with particular practices mediate and bridge the cultural-transcendent levels of human relations as a substantive spirituality. Some individuals may participate in practices drawn from one religious tradition for a functional effect, such as yoga or mindfulness, while participating substantively in a different tradition. Educating students on the traditions that functional practices come from can provide an opportunity for appreciation of the tradition as well as an opportunity to discuss potential cultural misappropriation.

The use of mediating language requires imagination. In fact, imagination and openness are necessary to gain the benefit of Berling's transformative learning process in encountering difference or entering other worlds, including understanding a spiritual domain. Transformation occurs because of our ability to imagine alternative ways of being in relationship with one another.[26] Imagination, shaped by physical, psychological, cultural, and spiritual relationships, is the interpretive lens of our experience. The imagination connects us to reality in terms of self-understanding, cultural identities, and our individual values or faith as a framework of reliance. From our imagination, we interpret experience, determine its significance, and give that experience personal, cultural, and spiritual meaning. It fashions and carries the pursuit of our passions.

---

[25] See Kim, 21.

[26] Berling, 28, and therein 26–27, citing, Maxine Greene, *Releasing the Imagination: Essays on Education, the Arts, and Social Change* (San Francisco: Jossey-Bass, 1995), 3. Experiences are transformative when something new emerges through a transcendent connection. See, generally, Graves. The Civil Rights era demonstrates that real change came about because of the shifts in dominant culture boundaries and individual willingness to engage in ongoing, unifying practices across difference, whether the context for those practices was religious or secular.

Critical for understanding, imagination also allows us to have empathy for one another while still acknowledging significant differences, providing formative community.[27]

Spiritual imagination produces the wisdom found in religious and non-religious traditions of human flourishing, such as stories passed down in families, stories surrounding national figures or holidays, the Twelve Steps, the teachings of Jesus or Buddha, or pan-Native American traditions. To better understand how integral our imagination is to our sense of self, García-Rivera describes the relationship between our imagination and reality as our imaginal existence.[28] Personal reality consists of the composition of our imaginal existence and changes depending on how open or closed its doors are.

For example, if I have a meaningful relationship with Jesus, a Buddha, or the homeless man at the corner and they occupy some part of my imaginal existence, then each of these figures is significant and real to me. I am more aware of social behaviors that support or attack Christianity, Buddhism, or efforts to end homelessness and more likely to take action. If I have no such relationships, then neither Jesus, a Buddha, nor the homeless man will be part of my imaginal existence or my reality. Because of imaginal existence, dismissing someone's interpretation of their cultural and transcendent connections can effectively diminish their hope, their humanity, and their sense of personhood.[29] Further, such dismissal can be interpreted as disrespectful or disempowering to an individual's voice and agency, which can negatively impact relations in any number of settings, from business or healthcare to educational, religious, or vocational.

A Bi-focal View

Embedded within the definition of spirituality, above, and the discussion of transcendent-level connections, lies one of Berling's preferred learning

---

[27] Berling, 39–40.

[28] Alejandro García-Rivera, *St. Martin de Porres: The "Little Stories" and the Semiotics of Culture* (Maryknoll, NY: Orbis Books, 1995), 102–5.

[29] Berling, 72–73. As Berling emphasizes, understanding is enhanced when one has a clear sense of one's own identity and is not overwhelmed by uncertainty in learning of other traditions nor so rigid that forming relationships becomes difficult.

tools: bi-focal perspectives of the synoptic vision and the local context.[30] García-Rivera, a colleague of Berling's, referred to these perspectives as the particularized identity and the larger, encompassing whole, or ultimate reality. As articulated at the level of the local context, the particularized identity comes through individual "little stories," revealing or pointing to the encompassing whole, or "big story."[31]

Keeping these two perspectives in mind helps in understanding the relationship between the intersectionality of the individual in a particular environment and a greater whole. Students who participate in a religious tradition may have a "default" synoptic vision to rely on, while nonreligious students may rely on national or cultural narratives that evince transcendent values. Reflecting on both perspectives allows students to intentionally consider how their interpretation of their individual life experiences may be congruent with a broader narrative or not.[32] A lack of congruity may be an opportunity to recognize possible hypocrisy at a broader level or an opportunity for reassessment of one's actions and beliefs in terms of Berling's second pole of learning.[33]

Bi-focal perspectives can be more easily integrated into curricula across multiple disciplines through wisdom sharing. Wisdom provides a relational, imaginative link between the particularized identity or the local context and a greater whole or synoptic vision.[34] Moreover, wisdom sharing as an experiential, reflective, and interpretive practice allows for individuals to speak of beliefs and practices that are life-giving and meaningful, although they may come from different traditions. This use of wisdom sharing draws from García-Rivera's interfaith aesthetics.

Interfaith aesthetics offers a variation for reflecting on the synoptic vision and local context through the concept of beauty.[35] García-Rivera asserts that conflict among people of different faiths and religions finds its source in what we conceive as good and true on a transcendent level expressed through theology and associated with particular religious

---

[30] Berling, 53.

[31] García-Rivera, 2.

[32] García-Rivera, 102–5.

[33] Berling, 71.

[34] Guorong, 443.

[35] Alejandro García-Rivera, "Interfaith Aesthetics: Where Theology and Spirituality Meet," in *Exploring Christian Spirituality: Essays in Honor of Sandra M. Schneiders, IHM*, ed. Bruce H. Lescher and Elizabeth Liebert (Mahwah, NJ: Paulist Press, 2006), 178–93.

identities. Thus, the particular points to and reveals trust in a greater whole. However, rather than attempting a unity of shared beliefs in connecting the particular to a greater whole, an aesthetic approach strives to find what is admirable in what the other finds beautiful in that connection to the whole. The dynamic of finding the admirable in the sacred presence of another's culture or tradition fosters relationship, and it can lead to an experience of love. An aesthetic approach accepts that people of varying religious, non-religious, and secular beliefs, sharing a common humanity, all belong to a greater whole beyond the particular. A sense of beauty or non-conceptual unity embraces this greater whole of our humanity. Conversely, García-Rivera notes that a number of deep thinkers across history find that trust in a tradition or authority without an experience of love only leads to conflict.[36] In a similar way, wisdom sharing does not demand a unity of shared beliefs and looks for appreciation in that which the other identifies as bearing or evidencing wisdom.

Accountability

The last pedagogical tool from Berling's approach discussed here is perhaps the most important in terms of addressing the challenges of higher education curriculum development across disciplines. Without a method of accountability, the need for spirituality and wisdom, let alone theology and religious studies, outside of the religiously affiliated private university becomes less credible.[37] Berling underscores the dynamic quality of learning across difference by instilling accountability into the process through transformation. In the acculturation of the learning process, where differences are recognized and cultural boundaries are crossed, engagement leads to relationships. For those relationships to

---

[36] García-Rivera, "Interfaith," 189–91. García-Rivera gives the following example of interfaith aesthetic. As the Christian can admire an ancient, hand-crafted tea bowl and its expression of the Buddhist non-duality of self, the Buddhist can admire a painting of spiraling colors and its expression of the reach of God's love. Faith continually forms through the aesthetic experience of love that connects the particular to a greater whole. Similarly, in the example of interfaith aesthetics, a true sharing in the non-conceptual unity of beauty results in admiration if not love for that which is loved by another.

[37] Berling, 36–37, citing, Jonathan Z. Smith, *Imagining Religion: From Babylon to Jonestown* (Chicago: University of Chicago Press, 1982), 21. The lack of attention in religious studies and theology to cultural and historical patterns and systems has been noted.

be enduring, an experience of transcendent connections must be transformational, resulting in a new *habitus*.[38] An evaluation of the student's spirituality in terms of new expressions of community, passion, and hope and transcendent connections also makes the learning process capable of assessment.[39]

Given the interdisciplinary nature of Berling's approach, in order to translate an acculturation experience through a framework of spirituality and wisdom sharing into a higher education curriculum, faculty and academic committees must be willing to prioritize student engagement with experiences of encountering difference and create the environment in which these experiences can occur. In fields unrelated to theology and religious studies, more specific materials and training for faculty would need to be developed along with intentional communication across disciplines and departments to emphasize this type of learning. An adaptation of wisdom sharing and the pedagogical tools could be integrated into other disciplines through course design.[40] Discussing the spirituality and wisdom of scientists, mathematicians, and social scientists whose methods are used in a classroom need not become overly burdensome to instructors; such discussions can open windows for students to a more comprehensive awareness of reality.

If we want to create space where authentic dialogue can take place across historical, cultural, spiritual and religious differences, the tools to do so must be integrated throughout our institutional learning systems, both public and private. Assuming a curriculum committee has approved an acculturative learning pedagogy, once faculty receive training, the pedagogical tools can easily be practiced either inside or outside the classroom as an ongoing assignment. Giving direction on the focus of self-reflection and a framework for interpretation that can be shared

[38] Berling, 52, 56, and citing at 57–58, Paul F. Knitter, "Beyond a Mono-Religious Theological Education," in *Shifting Boundaries: Contextual Approaches to the Structure of Theological Education*, ed. Barbara G. Wheeler and Edward Farley (Louisville: Westminster John Knox Press, 1991), 151, 162. This form of accountability in a spirituality framework will be marked by, at the very least, humility.

[39] It is likely that a self-assessment measurement could be conducted along the lines of the Functional Assessment of Chronic Illness Therapy-Spiritual Well-Being (FACIT-SP) which assesses for satisfaction in beliefs and relationships in coping with illness. See www.facit.org.

[40] Berling, 22–25, 63, discusses Paulo Freire, bell hooks, and Mary Boys as contributing to her thought process.

with a classmate provides the basis for an effective experience for students. Requiring a short, written statement and following up with a class discussion allows students to further identify what language best resonates with their perceived faith. While this practice may seem to fit more easily in a religious studies, cultural studies, or other humanities class, it can also be carried out effectively in an accounting, engineering, or criminal justice class. In my own work, I have used a spirituality framework in well-received presentations with religious and non-religious audiences in the fields of public behavioral health, nursing, youth substance abuse prevention, religious studies, and legal advocacy.

CONCLUSION

By using a framework of critical spirituality and articulating traditions of human flourishing through wisdom sharing, we can provide a means for students to better understand themselves and be open to better understanding others who hold different views or come from different life experiences. Through Berling's foundational approach to interreligious learning, we have the tools of mediating language, a bi-focal view, and accountability to equip our students and faculty in order to positively impact higher education curriculum development.

Our society is in a period of transition, in terms of religious and non-religious identification and otherwise. As the racially identified "white" majority becomes a minority, the ways in which the current majority has shaped research, development, funding, policies, and decision-making in the humanities and sciences will change. Students across disciplinary fields who identify with the current racial majority and its social privileges will need to be able to authentically relate to those with racial, ethnic, and cultural differences.[41] As a country that has long submerged its complicated pluralistic history in favor of a simpler story of the dominant culture's experience of the American Dream, we need a national reassessment and a new *habitus*, one that can more adequately engage the intersectionality of our students and their "multi-faith pluralism."[42]

---

[41]These cultural differences include age, sex, gender, disability, and addressing social conditions.

[42]See Berling, citing Knitter, 57–59.

BIBLIOGRAPHY

Ardelt, Monika. "Empirical Assessment of a Three-Dimensional Wisdom Scale." *Research on Aging* 25, no. 3 (2003): 273–84.

———. "Wisdom and Expert Knowledge System: A Critical Review of a Contemporary Operationalization of an Ancient Concept." *Human Development* 47 (2004): 257–85.

Berling, Judith. *Understanding Other Religious Worlds: A Guide for Interreligious Education.* Maryknoll, NY: Orbis Books, 2004.

Chatwood, Susan, Francois Paulette, et al. "Approaching Etuaptmumk: Introducing a Consensus-Based Mixed Method for Health Services Research." *International Journal of Circumpolar Health* 74 (2015). Accessed January 13, 2018. https://doi.org/10.3402/ijch.v74.27438.

Connolly, William. "Europe: A Minor Tradition." In *Powers of the Secular Modern: Talal Assad and His Interlocutors*, edited by David Scott and Charles Hirschkind, 75–92. Palo Alto, CA: Stanford University Press, 2006.

García-Rivera, Alejandro. *St. Martin de Porres: The 'Little Stories' and the Semiotics of Culture.* Maryknoll, NY: Orbis Books, 1995.

———. "Interfaith Aesthetics: Where Theology and Spirituality Meet." In *Exploring Christian Spirituality: Essays in Honor of Sandra M. Schneiders, IHM*, edited by Bruce H. Lescher and Elizabeth Liebert, 178–93. Mahwah, NJ: Paulist Press, 2006.

Gelpi, Donald. *The Gracing of Human Experience: Rethinking the Relationship Between Nature and Grace.* Collegeville, MN: The Liturgical Press, 2001.

Graves, Mark. *Mind, Brain, and the Elusive Soul: Human Systems of Cognition and Spirituality.* Burlington, VT: Ashgate Publishing, 2008.

Kim, David Kyuman. *Melancholic Freedom: Agency and the Spirit of Politics.* New York: Oxford University Press, 2007.

Lemmons, Willem. "Hume and Spinoza on the Emotions and Wisdom." *Scottish Journal of Philosophy* 3, no. 1 (2005): 47–65.

O'Brien, Suzanne Crawford, ed. *Religion and Healing in Native America: Pathways to Renewal.* Westport, CT: Praeger Publishers, 2008.

Stewart III, Carlyle F. *Black Spirituality and Black Consciousness: Soul Force, Culture and Freedom in the African-American Experience.* Trenton, NJ: Africa World Press, 1999.

Tagalik, S. *Inuit Qaujimajatuqangit: The Role of Indigenous Knowledge in Supporting Wellness in Inuit Communities in Nunavut.* National Collaborating Centre for Aboriginal Health. Prince George, BC: University of Northern British Columbia, 2009.

Tilley, Terrence. *Faith: What It Is and What It Isn't.* Maryknoll, NY: Orbis Books, 2010.

Townes, Emilie. *In a Blaze of Glory: Womanist Spirituality as Social Witness.* Nashville: Abingdon Press, 1995.

Turner, Nancy, Marianne Boelscher Ignace, and Ronald Ignace. "Traditional Ecological Knowledge and Wisdom of Aboriginal Peoples of British Columbia." *Ecological Applications* 10, no. 5 (October 2000): 1275–87.

Yang, Guorong, "Transforming Knowledge into Wisdom: A Contemporary Chinese Philosopher's Investigation." *Philosophy East and West* 52, no. 4 (October 2002): 441–58.

CHAPTER 8

Frames and Metaphors for Interreligious Dialog and the Interdisciplinary Study of Religion

Bonnie Howe

Abstract Judith Berling taught that it would be wise to consider carefully how we are thinking, to ponder what we are trying to do in religious studies. Bonnie Howe takes on this challenge by exploring how the metaphors and conceptual frames we use to think and talk about religion and interdisciplinary study shape our work. She explains how metaphors and frames open up, guide, constrain, and help validate the interdisciplinary study of religions.

Keywords Conceptual metaphor · Semantic frame · Category structure · Conceptual blending

Now more than ever, the world needs to understand religion and religions, plural. For the well-being and safety of humanity and the planet, deeper religious understanding is crucial. The thesis of this chapter

B. Howe (✉)
New College Berkeley, Berkeley, CA, USA

107
J. E. S. Park and E. S. Wu (eds.), *Interreligous Pedagogy*, Asian Christianity in the Diaspora, https://doi.org/10.1007/978-3-319-91506-7_8

is this: Deeper understanding can come from paying attention to the metaphors by which we live within our home religious traditions and communities, in the academic study of religion, and in interreligious encounters. Metaphors are keys that can unlock doors to interreligious dialogue and study because our metaphors display our core values and deepest commitments. They also map our fears and blind spots. Our attempts at understanding, dialog, and peacemaking will succeed or fail depending on our grasp of and fluency in our own and one another's conceptual metaphors.

The aim of this chapter is to explain how metaphors and the semantic frames that shape them matter in interreligious encounters and in the study of religion. There is no such thing as a *mere* metaphor. In fact, metaphors are *conceptual*. Metaphors both display and shape our thoughts in patterned, structured ways. According to evidence amassed by cognitive linguists and psychologists, metaphors are structured by conceptual and semantic frames.[1] Attention to conceptual and semantic framing can reveal patterns and connections among metaphors that we might otherwise miss. Frame-shaped metaphors carry emotional and logical valence; they can spin a message or prime people's responses, leading them toward drawing particular conclusions. The claim that we think with metaphors is a key argument of cognitive linguists, as is the notion that *metaphorical framing effects* can powerfully influence how people approach social problems and policies. For example, in a Stanford cognitive psychology study, subjects had markedly different responses to policy proposals for addressing crime, depending on whether they had been prompted beforehand to think about viruses or predatory animals.[2] Subjects who had seen the word "virus" flashed on a screen chose policies guided by the metaphor, CRIME IS AN EPIDEMIC. That is, they drew on the frames of epidemiology or public health as they selected their preferred responses to crime. But responses both at the personal level

---

[1] *Frames* are "structured understandings of the way aspects of the world function." Gilles Fauconnier and Eve Sweetser, *Spaces, Worlds, and Grammar* (Chicago: University of Chicago Press, 1996), 5.

[2] Paul H. Thibodeau and Lera Boroditsky, "Metaphors We Think with: The Role of Metaphor in Reasoning," *PLOS ONE* 6, no. 2 (2011): e16782, Stanford, CA: Department of Psychology, Stanford University, http://lera.ucsd.edu/papers/crime-metaphors.pdf. And see Benjamin Bergen, *Louder Than Words: The New Science of How the Mind Makes Meaning* (New York: Basic Books, 2012).

and to policy proposals were substantially different when the prompting word was "beast." With this framing prompt, participants were more likely to reason that criminals ought to be *hunted down* and *caged*. In fact, the researchers found that shifts in metaphor are often accompanied by shifts in policy. The realm of religion is full of metaphors that have equally divergent and potentially significant entailments. Inquiring minds and proponents of interreligious dialogue, then, will want to know more about metaphors and framing effects.

Defining Metaphor and Frame

Metaphors are more than mere poetic embellishments or rhetorical tactics. Cognitive linguists have found that metaphors are ubiquitous in both formal and everyday language, both spoken and written. Linguist George Lakoff and philosopher Mark Johnson define conceptual metaphor this way: The essence of metaphor is understanding and experiencing one kind of thing in terms of another.[3] That is exactly what we do when we study religions and engage in interreligious dialog and encounter. We use what we know from experience of one kind of thing—such as solving a math problem—to understand and experience another kind of thing, such as facing an impasse in interreligious understanding. Metaphors permeate the language we use, our academic disciplinary and interdisciplinary vocabulary, and our descriptions of what we are trying to do in our studies and dialogs.

Beginning with Blocks and the Purple Book

If we want to understand how metaphors and semantic frames shape interdisciplinary study and interreligious dialogue, we may as well start with Legos and *The Purple Book*.[4] "The Purple Book" is the affectionately adopted, alternative title Judith Berling's graduate students have given to her benchmark book, *Understanding Other Religious Worlds*. Here at the outset, observe that *"Religious Worlds"* uses a metaphor: RELIGIONS ARE WORLDS. The practices and rites, commitments and beliefs

---

[3] George Lakoff and Mark Johnson, *Metaphors We Live By* (Chicago: University of Chicago Press, 1980, 2003), 5. Emphasis theirs.

[4] Judith A. Berling, *Understanding Other Religious Worlds: A Guide for Interreligious Education* (Maryknoll, NY: Orbis Books, 2004).

of a given religion are compressed into an imaginary *world*. Of course, the religious universe is larger than any one such world; there are *other* religious worlds. We can play with this metaphor. It could evoke pictures of appreciative beholding from respectful distance but also invites visions of exploration and even of trans-world communication. That is the work Berling invites us to ponder and to take on, and for which she offers guidelines and models in *The Purple Book*. She even offers building blocks for that work.

Once upon a time, Judith Berling tells us in *The Purple Book*, there was a remarkable session of the Graduate Theological Union doctoral seminar on interdisciplinarity. On this day, a team of students divided the class into working groups at four small tables. Upon each table was a pile of Lego blocks. Each team was asked to use the blocks to build a model of interdisciplinarity. Everyone got busy. The student leaders roamed, observing the groups' interactions and problem-solving styles. In time, each group built a unique model of interdisciplinarity with their Lego blocks. No two Lego structures were alike.

What does this story tell us? Obviously, there is more than one way to envision interdisciplinarity. One could safely predict that if this Lego task were given to many, many sets of small groups, each group would build a unique model. But perhaps the most fascinating outcome is that none of the groups that day shared with or borrowed blocks from other groups. Even students in the seminar on interdisciplinary study of religion stayed within the boundaries of their assigned groups and accepted the assignment and materials as given. It was as though they assumed their groupings and assigned tasks were like long-established institutional departments, with their research agendas, norms, and procedures.

Frame and metaphor analysis predicts that something in the way the students individually and in groups conceptualized their tasks lent helpful structure but at the same time constrained and even skewed the outcomes of their work together. To understand how that works, it is helpful to look even more closely at semantic frames and conceptual metaphors, and to think about how they are related.

Sesame Street and the Logic of Frames and Metaphors

The terminology of "frames" and "framing" is tossed about in academic circles and in public discourse these days, usually without a clear definition. There is a technical definition, however, in the social sciences. The sociologist Erving Goffman first identified certain patterned phenomena and presented a model for frame analysis.[5] Crucially, Goffman noted that meaning was keyed to the frame being used. A *question* is understood differently in the frame of an oral exam rather than the frame of an everyday conversation. That is, oral exams are not ordinary conversations; these are separate *frames.* Goffman noted, too, that there are often multiple frames operating at the same time in any given situation or interaction. The Berkeley cognitive semanticist Charles Fillmore adopted and adapted this sociological model to study linguistic meanings. Fillmore defines **frame** this way:

> A system of categories structured in accordance with some motivating context.

> Any system of concepts related in such a way that to understand any one of them you have to understand the whole structure in which it fits.[6]

Some synonyms for Fillmore's semantic frames are "scripts," "scenarios," "idealized cognitive models," or "schematic representations of situation types."[7] For our purposes, it is important to note that various "models" of interdisciplinary studies can function as frames of the sort Goffman and Fillmore describe. Now, to grasp the possibilities for frame-shaped dialog and learning, look for a moment at how frames are used in another educational setting: Sesame Street.

"Waiter, there's a fly in my soup!" cries a grumpy old man sitting at a table with a place setting. In comes Grover, holding a serving tray; he is the waiter.[8] Viewers of this Muppets skit who have had similar real-life experiences know that if the customer orders soup, there is going to be a bowl and a spoon. How do they know that? These, Fillmore would say, are frame elements—props and roles belonging to a Restaurant frame. Even a child who had never been to a restaurant could learn some basic elements of a Restaurant frame from watching this skit.

---

[5] See Erving Goffman, *Frame Analysis* (Cambridge, MA: Harvard University Press, 1974).

[6] Charles Fillmore, "Frame Semantics," in *Linguistics in the Morning Calm* (Seoul: Hanshin Publishing, 1982), 111.

[7] Charles Fillmore, "Frames and the Semantics of Understanding," *Quaderni di Semantica* 6 (1985): 223.

[8] Sesame Street: Grover and a Fly in My Soup. YouTube video, running time 3:14, published (August 8, 2008), accessed February 1, 2018, https://www.youtube.com/watch?v=1C8nl8eBoq0.

Fillmore's point is that when we encounter a text or a painting, a movie or a dialog, our minds need only *one* element of a basic script or scene for the whole frame to be evoked. That is, frames are gestalts; a whole frame is basic and the parts depend on it. Because of the gestalt nature of the frame, as soon as one element is presented, the rest of the elements become available immediately as tools for thinking and talking about what's happening. Cognitive linguists have found that such frames are at work ubiquitously and systematically in our everyday language use. Or to put it another way, "people understand things by performing mental operations on what they already know."[9] The prefabricated structure of a frame facilitates the processing of new experiences and information quickly. Such alternative framings can radically change thinking processes, including assessing and reasoning in any given content.

Here is how frames and metaphors are connected: Conceptual metaphors use elements, roles, and actions from different semantic frames to help us *understand and experience* one kind of thing in terms of another. When the Stanford study subjects mentioned above saw "virus" before they read a crime report, the frames of Epidemics or public health problems were opened up and available. Many of them then reasoned about crime (the Target frame) using that public health Epidemic (Source) framing. Reasoning from the Source frame was shaping their reasoning about the Target—and in a one-way fashion. That is, they did not begin to use crime to reason about viruses. The same phenomenon arose with the subjects who read the same crime report but saw the word "beast" before they read the report. These people drew from their understanding and experience of wild animals, predators (Source frame), as they responded to the crime story (Target frame). For them, CRIMINALS ARE PREDATORS. Metaphors and frames, then, work hand in hand.

Back to the Seminar

Cognitive linguists and psychologists would say that the Lego block exercise was prompting students to identify and display their *framing* of interdisciplinarity and to display the conceptual metaphors they found most salient. Tellingly, they came up with multiple models, displaying multiple frames and metaphors for the interdisciplinary study of religion.

---

[9]Charles Fillmore, "Introduction to Framenet," PowerPoint Presentation, https://framenet.icsi.berkeley.edu/fndrupal/CJFFNintroPPT.

Later in the seminar, Professor Berling presented a taxonomy of eight models of interdisciplinarity. Students were encouraged to identify which model fit what they were doing presently in their research projects as well as which other models might augment or refine their work. Here are the eight models:

Discipline of Orientation/Home Discipline
Balanced Model
Interstitial Model: Working at or between the Boundaries
Emerging Conversation (Paris Café)
Problem/Issue-based Model
(Picture) "Frame" Model
Weaving Model
Thematic Overlapping Model[10]

Each of the eight models is anchored in a semantic frame just as surely as a Restaurant frame anchors that Sesame Street skit. These models become *metaphors* when we use them as anchor (Source) frames to understand and experience something else, such as interdisciplinary studies or interreligious dialogue. Cognitive linguists would name the metaphors INTERDISCIPLINARY WORK IS WEAVING; or INTERDISCIPLINARY STUDY IS PROBLEM-SOLVING; INTERDISCIPLINARY STUDY [or INTERRELIGIOUS DIALOGUE!] IS AN EMERGING CONVERSATION.

SIGNPOST: FRAMES AND METAPHORS AHEAD

Now—as Berling would surely agree—the List of Eight is not an exhaustive list. Interdisciplinary scholars of religion and people engaging in interreligious dialogue use lots of frames and metaphors. In what follows, I am going to focus primarily on the List of Eight, but I must mention a few additional key frames and metaphors that are also crucial in both interdisciplinary studies and in interreligious dialog. Readers will want to notice which metaphors and frames fit or clash with their own approaches; they may want to note which models feel new but might be worth trying. For heuristic purposes, I am going to depart from the

---

[10] Philip Wickeri, "Towards a More Perfect Union," *Berkeley Journal of Religion and Theology* 2, no. 1 (2016): 47–68.

order in which Berling outlined the models and begin with the sixth item, the "Frame" Model.

Berling's Picture "Frame" Model vs Fillmore's Frames

We begin with the "Frame" Model because starting here can help us clarify the overlaps and differences between the Berling's schematic and what Fillmore meant by *frame*. In Berling's eightfold taxonomy, the "Frame" Model signifies the use of interdisciplinarity as window dressing or as the frame around a picture. This is a metaphor: INTERDISCIPLINARY STUDY IS A PICTURE FRAME. It can be detected when interdisciplinarity is invoked at the beginning and again at the end of a given essay, book, or presentation, but is scarcely employed in the body of the work. The metaphor is drawing from semantic frames in the domain of art in which an actual physical frame is used to highlight some aspect of a visual perspective. The "Frame" Model, then, uses that Fillmore-type semantic framing to build a metaphor for understanding interdisciplinary work.

This Picture "Frame" Model in the list of Eight may be an intermediate position on the spectrum that runs from strictly uni-disciplinary to multidisciplinary to truly interdisciplinary work. A claim often heard in academia is that X or Y discipline is already inherently interdisciplinary. Biblical studies, social ethics, psychology and sociology of religion, spirituality, and spiritual formation—practitioners in all of these fields say that their work is intrinsically interdisciplinary. But if these scholars then proceed to employ a single method of inquiry and evaluation, interdisciplinarity serves primarily as a kind of (metaphorical) "Frame" for their work.

The other seven models in the eightfold taxonomy also use semantic frames, as defined by Fillmore, and the rest of this essay will explain why and how that is so.

Using Frame Analysis to Explore the Balanced Model

Readers encountering the words, "Balanced Model," might see in their mind's eye a classic weighing scale, with a fulcrum and two pans. Cognitive linguists would say the word "balanced" evoked that visual image and the frames to which it belongs. Using this metaphor to describe an approach to scholarly work suggests a schema in which two disciplines are being used together, and the scholar wants to (metaphorically) "weigh" the ways those disciplines are employed. In fact, language of *weighing* and *measuring*, of *scales* and of *imbalance* are all triggers for this frame. Thus, review boards vetting dissertation proposals ask if the disciplines employed in the work are in *balance*, or if one receives *lighter* use and coverage. This frame naturally lends itself to that kind of evaluation and to dialectical analysis. But it is also quite limited. There are just two pans in this kind of scale.

A reader encountering the language of "Balance" or "Balanced" might see a tightrope walker using a horizontal bar to help her maintain equilibrium. In that case, it would be important to keep the bar steady, as Justin Lane suggests in his discussion of the complexities of interdisciplinary approaches to the study of religion:

> The science of religion is like walking a tightrope; this endeavor should be interdisciplinary, drawing between historians, anthropologists, psychologists, biologists, and all the scholars of religion participating within those dialogues (there may be others as well that I have forgotten). As we walk this tightrope, we go from observing religion to explaining it, testing predictions (i.e. hypotheses) and theories back and forth in order to generate new knowledge about our subject with the ultimate goal of explanation. Beneath this tightrope-walking scholar is a vast canyon of speculation. Just as a tightrope-walker needs a bar to keep their balance and steady themselves to mediate between their points, the interdisciplinary scholar also needs to steady themselves. Now, the question naturally arises: What is the bar for those of us who wish to study religion scientifically?[11]

In fact, Lane blends this tightrope-walking metaphor with a dialog frame and a spatial, topographical one, where the rope is stretched across a vast canyon of speculation. We'll have more to say about metaphors of conversation and of spanning gaps later. Here, let us simply notice that there is more than a single way to construe the framing and related metaphors in even this one model—the Balanced Model. Why does that matter? Because each frame carries a certain coherence and logic, the entailments

---

[11]Justin Lane, "Keeping the Bar Steady: The Complexities of Interdisciplinary Approaches to the Study of Religion," Web: The Religious Studies Project (April 23, 2015), http://www.religiousstudiesproject.com/2015/04/23/keeping-the-bar-steady-the-complexities-of-interdisciplinary-approaches-to-religion/.

will vary. We are drawing on that logic, relying on it in our work, when we use particular frames and metaphors.

Variation on Balance: Binocularity

Another metaphor for thinking about how two disciplines can be used in tandem is binocularity.[12] This conceptual metaphor —INTERDISCIPLINARY STUDY IS BINOCULAR VISION—relies on another basic metaphor, KNOWING IS SEEING. Each discipline becomes a (metaphorical) *lens* through which to (metaphorically) *view* the object or field of study. Binoculars allow 3-D vision in which two *fields* of view are blended. Thus, metaphorically, two disciplines or approaches might be used not just one at a time, but in tandem, to create a (metaphorical) *stereoscopic* picture. Cognitive linguists use the notion of **conceptual blending** to describe such a merging of distinct parts into a new whole.[13] Moreover, binoculars can be adjusted for *focus* and *field of view*. All of the italicized words above can trigger this frame. Still, there is a built-in constraint to this framing: the limitation entailed in the binary (*bi-* = two) language. Many scholars use more than two disciplines in their work. These scholars probably prefer, then, frames that allow them to think and talk about more than two disciplines at once.

Thematic Overlapping Model

Here is a model that has the potential to help us think about what it is like to work with multiple disciplines or religions. 3-D Venn diagrams sometimes are used to schematize Thematic Overlap. When we speak of disciplines *intersecting* or *overlapping*, cognitive linguists would say we are evoking rudimentary spatial frames.[14] Each discipline is a Zone, Space, or Container, and these might have different sizes. The *degree* or

---

[12] Norris Palmer, "Binocularity, Perspicacity and Interstitiality," Symposium lecture, Learning as Collaborative Conversation: Celebrating the Scholarship and Teaching of Judith Berling, Berkeley, CA, May 26, 2016, https://portal.stretchinternet.com/cluadmin/full.htm?eventId=285730&streamType=video.

[13] See Gilles Fauconnier and Mark Turner, *The Way We Think* (New York: Basic Books, 2002).

[14] See Annette Herskovits, *Language and Spatial Cognition* (Cambridge: Cambridge University Press, 1986).

size of overlap matters. But this model is not particularly good at describing what is happening in the areas of overlap. We may know that certain disciplines highlight the same themes, but how and why and what it might mean is not evident. So while it gives us a basic spatial schematic, this is not a very rich frame.

Weaving Model

The Weaving Model does provide a richer scenario than Thematic Overlapping. Many frame elements and roles immediately come into view: One can see a loom (which is a literal frame!) and imagine various disciplines providing warp and woof *threads* or even subdisciplines or models providing different *colors* and *textures*. Weavers move, they work; this is not a static model. Moreover, the product of the work is a textile, a *fabric*, and that has rich metaphorical value. *Patterns* are implied and depicted in this model. The Weaving Model lends itself to thinking about and talking about the work and products, the useful outcomes, of religious study and interdisciplinarity.[15]

Problem-based Model

The problem-based model for interdisciplinary scholarship relies on a problem-solving frame.[16] Religion scholars using this model may frame the focal object of their study as a problem, using that frame metaphorically now to understand and experience something in the interdisciplinary study of religion (or interreligious dialogue) as an activity with *finding a solution* or *answer* as the goal. A more specific subframe of math may even be used. What are the constraints here, though? Are all issues or matters of interest in religious study and dialog *Problems* that need to be *Solved*? Or are the scholars who prefer this model actually thinking less of a math problem than of a *predicament*—a more general kind of problem, to which the goal might be *resolution*? The analysts at *Framenet* describe the predicament frame this way: "An Experiencer is in

---

[15] For Philip Wickeri, this is a favorite frame, partly because he has grown to appreciate the artistry and craft of rugs and other textiles. Wickeri, "Toward a More Perfect Union."

[16] "Resolve-Problem," Framenet, accessed March 20, 2018, https://framenet2.icsi.berkeley.edu/fnReports/data/lu/lu12316.xml?mode=lexentry&banner=.

an undesirable Situation, whose Explanation may also be expressed."[17] Do we sometimes, then, in religious studies and interreligious dialogue feel that we face a difficult predicament, that we are working toward explanations that will help alleviate something undesirable (tension; discord; misunderstanding; and mistrust)? The potential emotional valence this framing carries is powerful.

Borrowing: Related Subframe of Problem-Solving

Borrowing is not on the list of Eight, but it is certainly a favorite metaphor in interdisciplinary studies. In the academy, we speak of disciplinary *toolkits*, and scholars often speak of "*borrowing* tools and methods" from other disciplines. In religious studies, we often borrow heavily from secular disciplines: the social sciences, history, and in my case, linguistics.

Indeed, INTERDISCIPLINARY WORK IS BORROWING is a common metaphor for efforts to find appropriate methods and metrics for a given project. Some metaphors are active here: IDEAS ARE TOOLS and ANALYTICAL MODELS ARE TOOLS.

Clearly, religion scholars who use this model are *borrowing* more than tools and methods. Is it not also sometimes the implied authority of mathematical and scientific rigor that is being borrowed? We attempt to borrow legitimacy and respect. This model has the potential to proliferate variations, multiple scenarios; it is rich in that way—and one suspects that it is used often for that very reason.

The cognitive linguists at *Framenet* have analyzed the borrowing frame. They note that borrowing is one version of a more basic scenario of temporary transfer.[18] In interdisciplinary studies, we talk about good and bad borrowing, of the necessity to take care when we *appropriate* and *adopt* or *adapt* analytical and heuristic models, and even descriptive language or terminology. Faithful, good borrowing entails acknowledging *sources* and (metaphorical) "indebtedness." There's an ethos entailed in the interdisciplinary borrowing frame: We aim for accurate and apt borrowing, but do we unconsciously drop the temporary aspect of this

---

[17] "Predicament," Framenet, accessed January 30, 2018, https://framenet2.icsi.berkeley.edu/fnReports/data/frameIndex.xml?frame=Predicament.

[18] "Borrowing," Framenet, accessed January 30, 2018, https://framenet2.icsi.berkeley.edu/fnReports/data/frameIndex.xml?frame=Borrowing.

conventional frame? Are we not actually intending to *keep* the model, terminology, or schematic and *not give it back*?

The Paris Café/Emerging Conversation Model

The Emerging Conversation is another favorite interdisciplinary studies metaphor, one that provides a conventional but rich scenario complete with roles and informal rules of engagement. One variation on this theme, the Paris Café, yields an attractive, urbane picture. Scholars cast themselves as having the leisure and means to sit beside the Seine and let the interdisciplinary conversation or the interreligious dialog emerge organically. Here there is little of the urgency or rigor entailed in the problem-solving model. The conversation itself is the thing—along with perhaps openness to whatever might emerge. In fact, this scenario uses a basic conversation frame, spinning out a novel extension to set it in a Paris Café.[19]

This is a beautiful picture, but I wonder: At the Paris Café, are the interlocutors informally *chatting*? Cognitive linguists studying conversation framing have noticed that purpose and topic are core frame elements.[20] In some of our work, it will be important to discern which subframe of communication or of conversation we are using. That is, are we having a discussion or a quarrel, a Chat or a Debate?[21] Linguists also observe that conversation carries with it certain expectations: The understanding that human discourse is informational; the Gricean axiom that we'll tell the truth; turn-taking practices; ways of managing multiple viewpoints. Religion scholars often use the conversation frame metaphorically. That is, the participants or interlocutors are academic disciplines, a discipline is an interlocutor (or participant) in a conversation. A scholar proposes to put two or more disciplines or methodologies *in dialog with* one another, for example, or to let (secular) linguistics methods *speak into* biblical corpus studies.

---

[19] Esther Pascual and Todd Oakley, "Fictive Interaction," in *Cambridge Handbook of Cognitive Linguistics*, ed. Barbara Dancygier (Cambridge: Cambridge University Press, 2019), 347–60.

[20] "Conversation," Framenet, accessed January 30, 2018, https://framenet2.icsi.berkeley.edu/fnReports/data/lu/lu9972.xml?mode=annotation.

[21] "Chatting," Framenet, accessed January 30, 2018, https://framenet2.icsi.berkeley.edu/fnReports/data/frameIndex.xml?frame=Chatting.

Conversation is a rich scenario with lots of potential, but there are drawbacks and limitations. The imaginary Paris Café setting implies that the participants could be from almost anywhere in the world, that many languages could be spoken, and that the topics could vary according to the whims of the conversation partners. If we apply it to the tasks of interreligious dialogue, there is the danger of displaying the very kind of elitism currently giving rise to populist backlash and distrust of academia. Can we really imagine that all the potential participants from the various religious worlds would be welcomed and heard at this table? Would Sunni and Shia interlocutors chat amiably with American Baptist Christians, Sikh women and indigenous shamans? Those conversations would need to be carefully planned, so mutual understanding and peaceful interaction might emerge. And in fact, Judith Berling does offer wisdom, drawn from her deep experience, toward that very end.

Containers and Spatial Frames—The Topographical, Spatial Models

Now we come to another family of models that rely on spatial concepts and draw on our experiences of bounded *zones* or *spaces*, of *crossing boundaries*, and of *navigating* or *orienting* ourselves in and across spaces, *topographies*. I am including the Interstitial Spaces model here as well because where there is an interstice, there is a *boundary* or space in-between. The language of working "in the margins" prompts us to think of frames that rely on boundaries or geographical zones. We might like the notion of being outside disciplinary boundaries, with the implied lack of narrow confines and constraints. Do scholars who wind up in interdisciplinary studies tend to color *outside the lines*? Are we Boundary Crossers and Bridge Builders? That last metaphor uses construction, building and engineering frames with hints of topographical traversal, Travel. Where there are disciplinary territories, there are gaps and attempts to forge links, build Bridges. All of these are metaphors grounded in semantic frames. We use them to think about our work, its challenges and potential.

Orientations, Homes, Journeys, and Map-making

Interdisciplinary scholars often speak of our primary disciplines as our home disciplines, and of interdisciplinary study as a journey to other territories (disciplines) for which we need (metaphorical) maps and Guides or Guidelines. This model combines spatial and locational framing with container metaphors to help us describe the work as movement across a metaphorical landscape. The home discipline is schematized as not just a rudimentary container, but a house—our house—the place where we belong and are known, to which we can return if all else fails or where we come to tell the tales of our quests, our journeys.

The list of Eight and the variations on those themes have become part of the IDS (interdisciplinary studies) language community's conventional lingo. They are some of our most widely used metaphors and frames in interdisciplinary studies because they provide places to stage and perform our work as well as ways to describe and evaluate it.

But as we have seen even in this brief survey, the Eight are not the only metaphors and models for interdisciplinary studies. If we attend to the language we use, we will notice some gardening or farming frames when we speak of *hybrids* or *cross-fertilization*. We sometimes use language of confluence, where we imagine that merging DISCIPLINES ARE STREAMS in conduits (or rivers). There, the mingling is so complete that below the confluence you would not be able to separate out the contributing ideas, models, and data from the source waters.

Moreover, it is instructive to consider what frames and metaphors interdisciplinary scholars tend *not* to use. We may speak of our work as sojourning through foreign lands, but we do not think of it as *tourism*—or as *conquering* or *annexing* those lands. We tend not to use Military or Battle framing, even for work that feels challenging. I suspect that is because we would rather eschew the destructive and deadly scenarios and entailments belonging to those frames. But I also cannot recall hearing a scholar speak of her interdisciplinary work as a *dance*. It could work; we could understand the use of such a metaphor—but it is not, so far as I know, in our conventional toolkit.

Interdisciplinary scholarship and interreligious dialog *require* the use of frames and conceptual metaphors. Frames lend structure to metaphors; they carry logic (i.e., they have logical entailments). Whether a metaphorical frame is conventional and straightforward or novel, elaborate, or extended, it will structure and display our thinking. This is true for all frames and metaphors, including those we use in academic work and in interreligious dialogue. We do not leave our disciplinary homes without metaphors and frames, and we cannot do our work without them.

BIBLIOGRAPHY

Bergen, Benjamin. *Louder Than Words: The New Science of How the Mind Makes Meaning*. New York: Basic Books, 2012.

Dancygier, Barbara, and Eve Sweetser. *Figurative Language*. Cambridge Textbooks in Linguistics. Cambridge: Cambridge University Press, 2014.

Fauconnier, Gilles. "Mental Spaces." Web: UC San Diego, Cognitive Science. http://www.cogsci.ucsd.edu/~faucon/BEIJING/mentalspaces.pdf.

Fauconnier, Gilles, and Eve Sweetser. *Spaces, Worlds, and Grammar*. Cognitive Theory of Language and Culture Series. Chicago: University of Chicago Press, 1996.

Fauconnier, Gilles, and Mark Turner. *The Way We Think: Conceptual Blending and the Mind's Hidden Complexities*. New York: Basic Books, 2002.

Fillmore, Charles. "Frame Semantics." In *Linguistics in the Morning Calm*. SICOL, Seoul International Conference on Linguistics, Linguistic Society of Korea. Seoul: Hanshin Publishing, 1982.

Fillmore, Charles. "Frames and the Semantics of Understanding." *Quaderni di Semantica* 6 (1985): 222–53.

Fillmore, Charles. "Introduction to Framenet." Powerpoint. Web: Framenet. https://framenet.icsi.berkeley.edu/fndrupal/CJFFNintroPPT.

Goffman, Erving. *Frame Analysis: An Essay on the Organization of Experience*. Cambridge, MA: Harvard University Press, 1974.

Herskovits, Annette. *Language and Spatial Cognition: An Interdisciplinary Study of the Prepositions in English*. Studies in Natural Language Processing. Cambridge: Cambridge University Press, 1986.

Lakoff, George, and Mark Johnson. *Metaphors We Live By*. Chicago and London: University of Chicago Press, 1980, 2003.

Lane, Justin. "Keeping the Bar Steady: The Complexities of Interdisciplinary Approaches to the Study of Religion." Web: The Religious Studies Project (April 23, 2015). http://www.religiousstudiesproject.com/2015/04/23/keeping-the-bar-steady-the-complexities-of-interdisciplinary-approaches-to-religion/.

Palmer, Norris. "Binocularity, Perspicacity and Interstitiality." Symposium lecture at Learning as Collaborative Conversation: Celebrating the Scholarship and Teaching of Judith Berling, Berkeley, CA, May 26, 2016. https://portal.stretchinternet.com/cluadmin/full.htm?eventId=285730&streamType=video.

Pascual, Esther, and Todd Oakley. "Fictive Interaction." In *Cambridge Handbook of Cognitive Linguistics*, edited by Barbara Dancygier, 346–60. Cambridge Studies in Linguistics. Cambridge: Cambridge University Press, 2017.

Thibodeau, Paul H., and Lera Boroditsky. "Metaphors We Think with: The Role of Metaphor in Reasoning." *PLOS ONE* 6, no. 2 (2011): e16782. Stanford, CA: Department of Psychology, Stanford University. Accessed October 15, 2017. http://lera.ucsd.edu/papers/crime-metaphors.pdf; https://doi.org/10.1371/journal.pone.0016782.

Wickeri, Philip. "Toward a More Perfect Union: The Contribution of Judith Berling to Religious Pluralism in Theological Education." Surjit Singh Lecture in Comparative Religious Thought. *Berkeley Journal of Religion and Theology* 2, no. 1 (2016): 47–68.

CHAPTER 9

Concluding Reflections

Judith A. Berling

Abstract Some of Judith Berling's pedagogical principles, which can be summarized as student-centered, collaborative, and engaged learning are not only embedded in all chapters but are also critically appropriated and creatively extended. Through Berling's own dialogue with each chapter, she explains what the essential notions of her pedagogy are and how her pedagogy is adapted and extended into her students' teaching or research fields. Understanding and negotiating difference, creating conversations and relationships across boundaries of difference, is one of the most important challenges in our diverse world. Berling concludes that the chapters in this volume explore how to foster such understanding, such conversations, and such relationships in both the classroom and in community-based research.

Keywords New learning environment · Student-centered learning
Collaborative learning

J. A. Berling (✉)
Graduate Theological Union, Berkeley, CA, USA

© The Author(s) 2018   125
J. E. S. Park and E. S. Wu (eds.), *Interreligous Pedagogy*, Asian Christianity
in the Diaspora, https://doi.org/10.1007/978-3-319-91506-7_9

It is heartening for me to see how my former students, now successful professionals, have consciously built upon some of the principles which I sought to instill in my seminars. They have developed them further, added new ideas, and carried them into new territories.

The pedagogical chapters in this book have all built on the principles of student-centered, collaborative, and engaged learning that empowers students' distinctive voices. But the authors have rightly and creatively adapted these principles, augmented and expanded them to meet the requirements of new student audiences and new learning environments.

Courtney Bruntz reaches out to millennial students with engaged and active learning that fits their styles and expectations. She adds the "flipped classroom" concept to my approach; the two are similar in many respects, so this fusion complements and strengthens my engaged and collaborative model. She creatively considers how best to make small group discussions work beyond a superficial level, setting up and developing thoughtful learning outcomes. She thinks through prior preparation and the structures of learning environments so that students get the very most out of the learning experiences that will engage their interests. Moreover, she consciously works against stereotypes, so that she can measure changes in attitudes and assumptions.

Jung Eun Sophia Park considers one particular group of millennials, the "Nones" or "spiritual but not religious," who can feel awkward or uncomfortable in traditional religion courses because they do not bring the language of any specific tradition. She turns to postcolonial and cultural critique to stretch her own pedagogical concepts and to understand the obstacles faced by "Nones" approaching courses too often structured around Christian and colonial understandings of "religion." She then uses Jacque Lacan's concept of gaze to create a "gaze model," which "is distinct in that the subject does not have any fixed position and the subject gains a certain level of knowledge of self and of the object(s) through the gaze. Nones can learn religions through gaze which emphasizes one's own unsatisfied desire for infinity and wisdom."

Those of us teaching religion increasingly struggle with how to teach both students who claim a tradition or traditions and the "Nones," questioning our own pedagogical assumptions and constructs and also seeking how to help students communicate and collaborate across the religious/none divide. Sophia Park's chapter can stimulate us to consider new approaches to this challenge.

Elizabeth Stanhope Gordon takes on another aspect of the not conventionally religious—students from the sciences and social sciences who bring secular assumptions and understandings into the classroom but who need nevertheless to understand the role of "religion" in society. She uses the notion of "mediating language," which I took from Kenneth Bruffee's work on collaborative learning, to seek conceptual approaches that mediate between "religious" and "secular" views. In her case, this means opting for "spiritual" rather than "religious," and for "wisdom sharing" rather than "interreligious learning." She is using the rising cultural trend of "spiritual but not religious" as an opportunity to articulate this mediating and bridging language. I believe this is a promising approach for institutions seeking to address "spiritual" values across the curriculum in the service of encouraging education of whole persons who can reflect on their higher values in an increasingly technologically-dominated world. I would only note that one approach to interreligious education (the challenge of understanding very different religious traditions) takes a similar tack: John Thatamanil of Union Theology Seminary in New York understands "theology" (a Christian-dominated term) as "embodied wisdom" and urges that students learn and practice the wisdom traditions of other religions as one mode of understanding.[1]

Emily S. Wu combines the principles of engaged pedagogy and collaborative learning with community-engaged Service-Learning, taking students into other cultural settings to learn, to develop relationships, and to serve. Service-Learning is a powerful pedagogy, particularly when it is well designed, as in Emily Wu's courses. In its early years, Service-Learning was too often simply required volunteerism, good for the growth of student maturity, responsibility, and general exposure to the world, but lacking specific cognitive learning outcomes. In Emily Wu's Service-Learning at Dominican University, the service to the community is also in service of the students' learning specific intercultural and communication skills and analyzing critical knowledge. I was particularly struck by one undergraduate's shock and delight that she could become a researcher, a knowledge producer, rather than a mere receiver of knowledge produced by others. This is engaged learning at its very best.

---

[1] "Integrating Wisdom: Comparative Theology as the Quest for Interreligious Wisdom," in *Experiments in Empathy for Our Time*, ed. Najeeba Syeed and Heidi Hadsell (In press).

Joanne Doi brings the methods of engaged and collaborative learning to complex issues of repressed historical memory and social justice in her course on Pilgrimage to Manzanar, the site of a Japanese internment camp. Joanne's course design is powerful because of her deep reflection about her stake in the course and her student-centered adaptability. She has deeply considered the forces that brought her to design the course—first her ministry among the Aymara in Peru, and then the powerful rediscovery of the memory of her own family's internment and how that has shaped her identity as an Asian American. She understandably designed the course originally for Japanese and Asian Americans to help them confront and understand that history. Then, when she drew a much wider range of students than she had anticipated, she used the frame of pilgrimage to construct a course that could have meaning for all participants, whether or not they were Asian or Asian American. She allowed for all of the students to explore, both spiritually and theologically, their own relationship to this history, to create a community of mutual understanding, shared spirituality, and shared visions of a more just society (including standing up against the Muslim bans). She also connected the students with survivors to learn and share their stories, much in the spirit of Emily Wu's students collecting oral histories of Vietnamese Americans. Such thoughtful collaborative and engaged learning not only creates profound understanding in the learners, but also creates relationships and the skills and sensitivities to create future relationships. It also strengthens learners' understandings of and commitment to address issues of social justice, past and present. To cite a concept used by Doi herself, it fosters what Johann Baptist Metz called "mysticism of open eyes, an increased readiness to perceive, to see more, not less, to name the visible and invisible suffering and pay attention to it, to be moved to compassion, to 'suffer with,' to be moved to respond."

Ofelia Villero is also deeply concerned with cultural sensitivity and social justice. As she describes in her chapter, she is one of two students out of nearly two hundred who took the seminar on course design, engaging deeply in all aspects of its learning, only to clarify that her vocation was to research and not to teaching. However, since she is deeply committed to community-based participation research, which gives agency and voice to community members as partners in creating culturally appropriate solutions to problems, she has found that the model of interreligious learning which I articulated in my book provides a useful framework for conceptualizing and explaining the process. Like Elizabeth Gordon, she works in a world dominated by the assumptions of the STEM fields, in this case a strong bias for quantitative data and a tendency to see human subjects as objects of research or "animals in the zoo." Like Elizabeth, she works hard to find mediating language and concepts to explain the importance of engaging the agencies, voices, and cultural particularities of the subjects of research, and thus of qualitative research methods. Her example of creating supportive care networks for Filipina women with breast cancer through engaged and collaborative community-based research is a wonderful example of collaborative and engaged learning adapted to a community-based participant research project. Understanding difference, honoring particularities and cultural sensitivities, are not merely progressive ideals, but important principles for solving problems in the real world—in this case how to lower mortality rates among Filipina women with breast cancer.

Bonnie Howe's chapter is a meta-reflection on issues behind constructing pedagogical approaches to help learners understand religions and religious difference. Bonnie's analysis of metaphors and frames is a challenge to teachers to be aware of their own pedagogical assumptions and to be alert to the assumptions of learners so that they can better negotiate issues of difference. Bonnie has built upon the meta-reflection that was core to the Interdisciplinary Studies Seminar, which asked students to probe behind the simple statement of their topic or interests, to understand their research questions, to think deeply about what disciplines and theories they would deploy to answer those questions, and then to consider the consequences and accountabilities of those choices. She cites the eight models of interdisciplinarity that were used when she took the seminar and unpacks the assumptions behind those models by naming the metaphors embedded in them. As the seminar evolved over more than twenty years, the number of models increased as students in each seminar proposed new ones, and increasingly students were urged to create an active rather than structural model, since unpacking the metaphors and images embedded in an active model helped them to discern what assumptions they were making about how they would go about the process of doing research. They were encouraged to create an active model that related to their own experiences and interests so that they would have a rich sense of what that activity entailed and thus could unpack the metaphor more fully.

Howe's analysis is helpful for anyone doing interdisciplinary research or teaching. We too often put aspects of disciplines together without thinking through the implications of the choices for our work or for our students. But it also can be applied to the language that we use to describe any course or learning assignment. It is challenging to become aware of the assumptions embedded in one's language and images—even in one's own discipline. When we teach students from other disciplines or from other cultural and socio-economic backgrounds, the assumptions carried in our language, metaphors, and images can be both alien and opaque to them. When students in our courses misconstrue or misuse the language and images we put before them and describe issues in language that seems "wrong" to us, we need to look at the assumptions embedded in the language used by both teacher and learners, in its metaphors and images, to see if we can identify the problem and create some mediating language to move toward common ground and, thus, begin a more fruitful conversation.

Understanding and negotiating difference, creating conversations and relationships across boundaries of difference, is one of the most important challenges in our diverse world. The chapters in this volume explore how to foster such understanding, such conversations, and such relationships in both the classroom and in community-based research. And they highlight the issues and assumptions that teachers and researchers must wrestle with in order to continually perfect their ability to cross boundaries and help others negotiate difference. This work is never done; it is an art that requires commitment and appropriate humility, a passion for listening to and engaging others in their fullness. I am deeply proud that my former students are taking on these issues with such passion and creativity, each doing their part to enhance the work of boundary-crossing and mutual understanding.

BIBLIOGRAPHY

Thatamanil, John. "Integrating Wisdom: Comparative Theology as the Quest for Interreligious Wisdom." In *Experiments in Empathy for Our Time*, edited by Najeeba Syeed and Heidi Hadsell. In press.

Index

Printed by Printforce, the Netherlands